Modern Primitive Quilts

Laurie Simpson

modern
Primitive
Quilts

Redefining Country Style

Acknowledgments

Thank you to:

✳ The entire staff of Martingale & Company® for unflagging support.

✳ Robin Fahmie and Julie Burns for allowing quilts from their collections to be photographed for this book.

✳ Rita Barnard for her support, advice, and for always lending a helping hand.

✳ Bonnie Smith for her beautiful drawings and cheerful support.

✳ Everyone at Lake Street Mercantile for help and encouragement.

✳ Polly Minick for her constant creativity, inspiration, and partnership.

✳ Bill and Lorelei for their love and understanding and the ability to put up with the flotsam and jetsam of a creative life.

Modern Primitive Quilts: Redefining Country Style
© 2007 by Laurie Simpson

That Patchwork Place® is an imprint of Martingale & Company®.

Martingale & Company
20205 144th Ave. NE
Woodinville, WA 98072-8478 USA
www.martingale-pub.com

Printed in China
12 11 10 09 08 07   8 7 6 5 4 3 2 1

Mission Statement
Dedicated to providing quality products and service to inspire creativity.

Credits
CEO: Tom Wierzbicki
Publisher: Jane Hamada
Editorial Director: Mary V. Green
Managing Editor: Tina Cook
Developmental Editor: Karen Costello Soltys
Technical Editor: Ellen Pahl
Copy Editor: Sheila Chapman Ryan
Design Director: Stan Green
Illustrator: Robin Strobel
Cover Designer: Stan Green
Text Designer: Regina Girard
Photographer: Brent Kane

Library of Congress
Cataloging-in-Publication Data
Library of Congress Control Number: 2006035732

ISBN: 978-1-56477-726-3

Contents

Introduction

I have loved old quilts, old fabrics, and old things all of my life. Old objects have been my source of inspiration since I began making quilts more than 30 years ago, and they are still my muse. These are the quilts I want to make and to live with. Antique folk-art textiles never disappoint me. Their care-free design and construction is refreshing. Perfection never seems to be a top priority in these designs. The maker's desire to create is the theme that comes out strong and clear. I can imagine the artists being moved to stitch by both a longing for lovely textiles and a need to tell their story. I have found I am no different. I am forever in debt to the fiber artists who have come before me.

Despite my love of old textiles, I don't ever want to abandon the luxury and ease of the twenty-first century. Central air, dishwashers, and books on CD are also a valued part of my life. My old-looking quilts reflect a primitive country style, but they have found the perfect niche in my modern home. The juxtaposition of soft, handmade textiles and clean, modern lines is a wonderful way to show off vintage quilts.

Since the quilting renaissance of the 1970s, historians and textile scholars have given us a wealth of information about old textiles, and fabric companies have filled the void with accurate reproduction fabrics such as calicoes, indigos, and shirtings. Many of us have made quilts with these riches and still long to make more. While I strive to tell my own stories in cloth, it is always with an old and homey patina. I have added a few techniques of my own to give my quilts the look of another time.

This collection of quilts and textiles is my response to filling that need to create. I hope the quilts inspire you to re-create them—and also to create some masterpieces of your own.

Yellow Work Chicken Sampler

This quilt pays homage to the many antique quilts with embroidered animals that I have seen and admired. It is stitched primarily by hand, using the English-paper-piecing technique.

Materials

All yardages are based on 42"-wide fabric.

6 yards *total* of assorted black prints for quilt top

1 yard of black star-print fabric for outer border and binding

⅓ yard of gold print for inner border

3 yards of fabric for backing

51" x 64" piece of cotton batting

670 paper hexagons*, 1" size

Chalk pencil

Yellow pearl cotton

Embroidery hoop

Appliqué pins

Freezer paper (5 squares, 14" x 14")

*Hexagon paper foundations can be found at your local quilt shop or online. See "Resources" (page 95) for further information. You can also make your own using the pattern (page 16).

Antique Look

I used matte pearl cotton called Homestead Cotton from Halcyon Yarns. I like this pearl cotton because it is not shiny and looks old to me. It is my choice when reproducing antique textiles.

Cutting

From the black fabrics, cut:

✳ 5 squares, 14" x 14" (for chicken embroidery backgrounds)

From the gold print, cut:

✳ 6 strips, 1½" x 42"; cut 2 of the strips in half to make 4 strips, 1½" x 21"

From the black star-print fabric, cut:

✳ 6 strips, 2½" x 42"; cut 2 of the strips in half to make 4 strips, 2½" x 21"

✳ 6 strips, 2¼" x 42"

From the backing fabric, cut:

✳ 2 pieces, 42" x 54"

Embroidering the Chicken Blocks

1. Using a light box and the chalk pencil, trace the chicken designs (pages 17–21) onto the black 14" squares. If you don't have a light box, you can tape the pattern to a window and trace.

2. Stitch the chickens using an outline stitch (stem stitch) and the yellow pearl cotton, referring to "Embroidery Stitches" (page 91). Press, using a pressing cloth, and set aside. Use other embroidery stitches as desired. Note that I used a feather stitch for the tail feathers of the chicken in the upper-left block.

Finished quilt: 47" x 59½"

Slow but Steady

Many people may think this quilt is overwhelming, but it will come together quickly if the stitching is done in stolen moments riding in the car, during your lunch hour, or while watching TV. Both the embroidery and the hexagon stitching are very portable.

Preparing the Hexagons

Use the pattern (page 16) if you choose to make your own hexagons. Cut them out of sturdy paper. Hexagons can be used again for other projects, but when they become too soft or lose their shape, it's best to discard them. You need a total of 670 hexagons.

From the 670 hexagons, crosscut:

✳ 28 half hexagons* (14 hexagons cut across the widest point)

✳ 60 half hexagons (30 hexagons cut across the shortest point)

✳ 2 quarter hexagons (1 hexagon cut in quarters; use the 2 lower quarters)

*Note: one half hexagon is extra; you need 27. You can use it for the quarter hexagons.

Hexagon cut across the widest point. Cut 14 to make 28.

Hexagon cut across the shortest point. Cut 30 to make 60.

Quarter hexagon. Cut 1 to make 1 of each.

1. Pin a paper hexagon foundation to the wrong side of a piece of black fabric. Fussy cutting is an option if there is a design that you want to highlight. One of the black prints that I used featured a gold star. I fussy cut the fabric to center the stars within the hexagon.

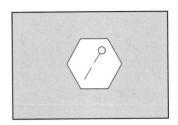

2. Trim around the hexagon, leaving a ¼" seam allowance. There is no need to measure each one—after a few you will cut accurately enough by eye.

¼"

3. Fold the seam allowances over the foundation to the back. Using a contrasting color of thread, baste the fabric to each hexagon. Begin and end your thread on the back. Take a stitch over each overlapping corner.

Making the Hexagon Frames

Once your paper hexagon pieces are all basted, you will assemble hexagon "frames" for the embroidered chickens. All fabric placement is random, so grab your hexagons without looking and sew them together.

1. Place two hexagons right sides together. Stitch them together along one side using a whipstitch. Insert the needle between the basted seam allowance and the paper foundation to

hide the knot. The whipstitch should just catch a few threads on the edge of each hexagon. Try not to stitch through the paper. To end the stitching, take two tiny stitches; then make a knot in a third stitch and cut the thread. Join four hexagons in a chain as shown. Make six of these four-hexagon units.

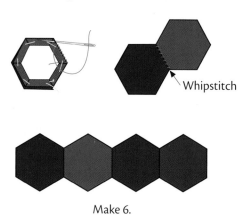

Whipstitch

Make 6.

2. Stitch the six units together as shown using a whipstitch.

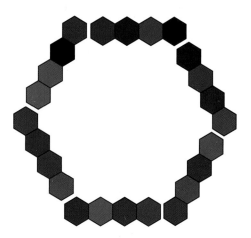

3. Stitch five hexagons together into a chain; make six of these units.

Make 6.

4. The five-hexagon units will be stitched to the frames made in step 2. To do this, align the end of a five-hexagon unit with a corner hexagon of a frame, right sides together, and whipstitch the first edge as shown.

Whipstitch edge.

5. Fold the five-hexagon unit back and it will line up with one side of the frame.

Whipstitch

6. This newly added unit will be sewn onto the frame using a nearly invisible ladder stitch. To do this, turn the frame over so that the wrong side is up. You will start on the right if you are right-handed. Insert your needle into the seam allowance and work one stitch

on one hexagon. Then move directly across and take another stitch; move directly across again. Once this sewing line is drawn taut, the stitches are practically invisible. At each intersection point, make an anchoring stitch and move on to the next segment. In this manner, stitch the unit to the existing frame.

Ladder stitch

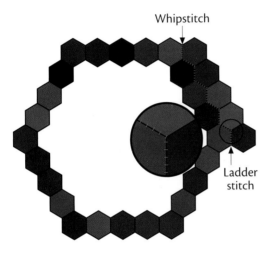

Whipstitch

Ladder stitch

7. When you come to the end of the segment, go back and take some ladder stitches in the other direction. Pull taut and tie a knot. This will anchor the stitches and bring the hexagons snugly together.

End by stitching in the opposite direction.

8. Attach all five-hexagon units this way until there is a double row of hexagons in the frame.

9. Stitch six hexagons together in a chain; make six of these units.

Make 6.

10. Using a whipstitch, and then a ladder stitch, attach these units to the frame as you did the previous units.

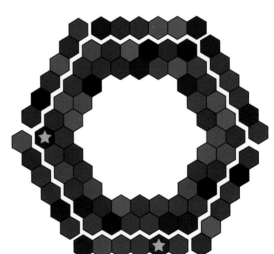

11. Repeat steps 1 through 10 to make four frames.

12. Repeat steps 1 through 8 to make a fifth frame for the center. Then stitch five hexagons together to make a chain. Repeat to make two five-hexagon chains and sew to the frame as shown.

Putting the Chickens into the Frames

1. Place a towel or soft cloth on your ironing surface and lay an embroidered chicken block right side down on top. Iron a 14" square of freezer paper, shiny side down, onto the wrong side of the chicken block.

2. Arrange each frame around a chicken and pin into place. Note that the frames should be positioned so that there is a peak at the top, with the chicken centered below the peak. Use the fifth frame around the center chickens.

   You'll notice in my quilt that the two embroidered chickens on the left appear to have circular backgrounds. That's because I discovered after appliquéing the frames to the chickens that the chickens were on an angle. I cut the embroidered chickens away, creating a circle, and then appliquéd them to a new

background piece. Feel free to do this if you like the look, but it's an extra step that you don't need to take.

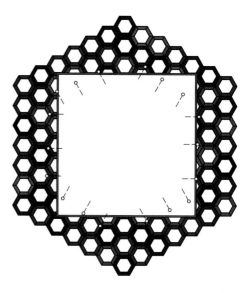

3. Take the units to the sewing machine and use a long basting stitch to stitch each frame onto a chicken through all the layers. Stitch approximately ½" from the inner edge of the frame.

4. Gently remove the freezer paper. Hand appliqué the edge of the frame onto the chicken block. Repeat for all five frames. Remove the basting stitches and set the blocks aside.

Assembling the Quilt Top

1. Using a whipstitch and a ladder stitch, make hexagon units as shown. These units will make up the rest of the quilt. Whipstitch hexagons and partial hexagons into chains, and then join the chains using a ladder stitch.

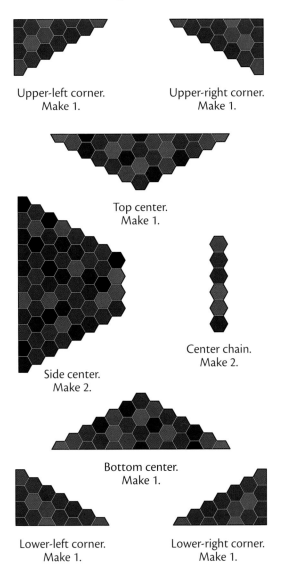

Upper-left corner.
Make 1.

Upper-right corner.
Make 1.

Top center.
Make 1.

Side center.
Make 2.

Center chain.
Make 2.

Bottom center.
Make 1.

Lower-left corner.
Make 1.

Lower-right corner.
Make 1.

2. Using the whipstitch and the ladder stitch, join the units to make the finished quilt referring to the quilt diagram. Add half hexagons to

the sides of the frame units as needed. Once all the half hexagons are added and the units are joined, you can clip the basting stitches and remove the paper hexagons.

3. Sew a 1½" x 21" gold print strip to each of the 1½" x 42" strips. Press. Measure your quilt top through the center and cut two strips to the exact length of your top. Sew these strips to the sides of your quilt top. I recommend sewing the inner borders on by hand since you will be dealing with so many seams. Press the seam allowances toward the strips.

4. Measure the width of your quilt top through the center and cut the two remaining gold print strips to the exact width of your quilt top. Sew these to the top and bottom of your quilt. Press the seam allowances toward the strips.

5. Sew a 2½" x 21" black strip to each of the 2½" x 42" black strips. Measure your quilt top as before to cut and add the two outer side

borders, and then the top and bottom borders. Press toward the outer border.

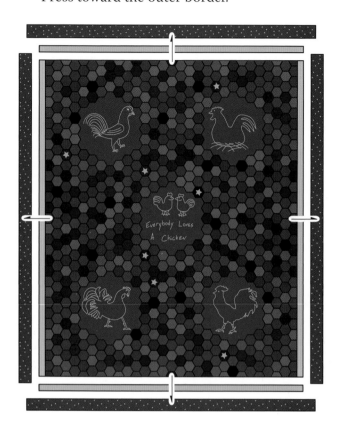

Finishing the Quilt

1. Remove the selvages from the backing fabric and join the pieces to make a piece approximately 54" x 81". Press the seam open.

2. Center and layer the quilt top and batting over the backing; baste the layers together and then quilt as desired. "Yellow Work Chicken Sampler" was quilted ¼" inside each seam line and a twisted cable was quilted in the border.

3. Trim the backing and batting even with the quilt top. Use the 2¼" x 42" black star-print strips to bind the quilt referring to "Binding" (page 93) for instructions.

4. Make a label and attach it to the back of your quilt.

Pattern is full-sized. Do not add seam allowance to paper.

1" hexagon
Cut 670.

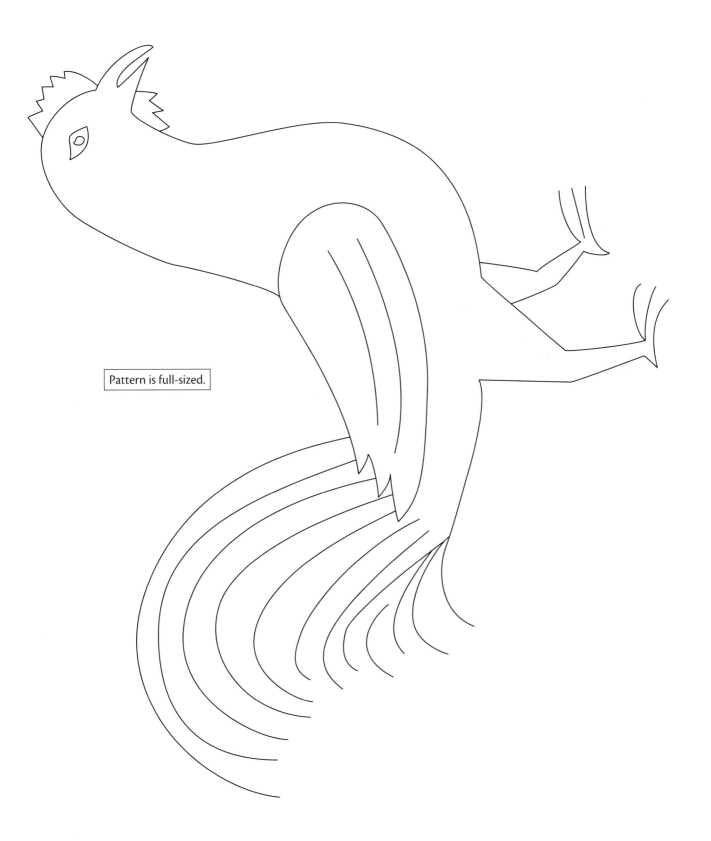

Pattern is full-sized.

Pattern is full-sized.

Patterns are full-sized.

Everybody Loves

A Chicken

Pattern is full-sized.

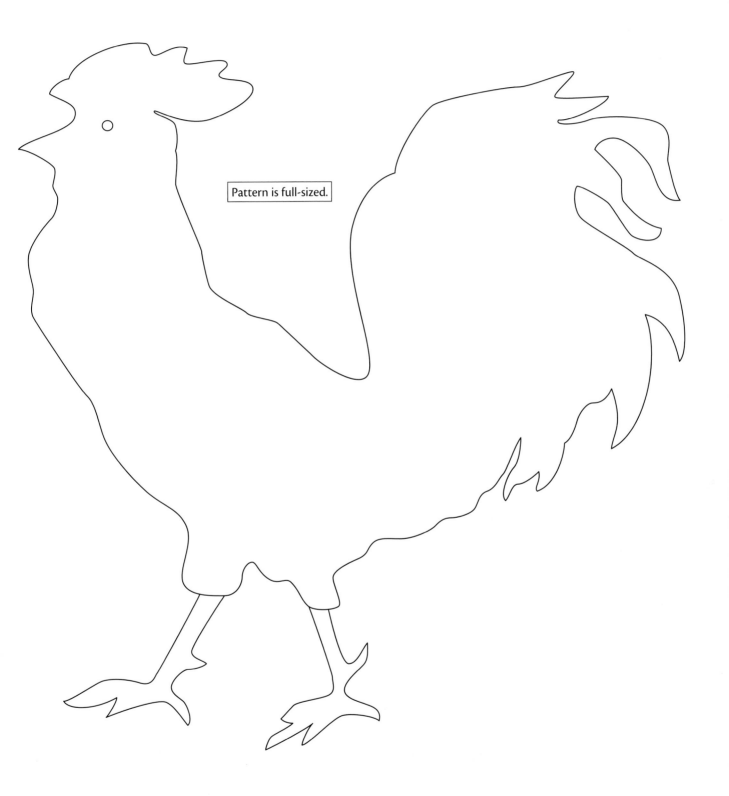

Pattern is full-sized.

Wild Wool Horses

This quilt combines my love of working with wool, my fondness for hand stitching, and of course my attraction to animals. I embellished the strip-pieced blocks with primitive embroidery—a common feature of many antique wool quilts.

Materials

All cotton yardages are based on 42"-wide fabric, and wool yardages are based on 54"-wide fabric. Wash and dry all wool fabrics before using.

2½ yards *total* of assorted neutral wools for pieced blocks

1½ yards *total* of assorted red wools for blocks and setting triangles

⅜ yard of black wool for horses

½ yard of cotton fabric for binding (optional)

3¼ yards of cotton fabric for backing*

55" x 55" piece of cotton batting

36 sheets of foundation-piecing paper**

Black pearl cotton or black tapestry wool

Freezer paper (4 squares, 11" x 11")

Fabric-glue stick

*The backing was folded to the front and also used for binding in the quilt shown. Select a backing fabric that coordinates with the front if you choose this method.

**I use computer paper or freezer paper, but commercially available foundation papers are much easier to tear away. See "Resources" (page 95).

Before You Begin

Refer to "Using Wool in Quilts" (page 86) for further information on purchasing, preparing, and working with this fabulous fabric.

Cutting

All measurements include ¼" seam allowances.

From the red wools, cut:

✳ 4 squares, 12½" x 12½"

✳ 2 squares, 18¼" x 18¼"; cut each square twice diagonally to make 8 triangles

✳ 2 squares, 9⅜" x 9⅜"; cut each square once diagonally to make 4 triangles

From the neutral wools, cut:

✳ 1½"- to 3½"-wide assorted strips. You will need strips that are approximately 4" to 10" long for the blocks, but the strips can be cut to the length needed during the piecing process.

Making the Blocks

1. Enlarge and trace the horse pattern (page 27) onto the dull side of each piece of freezer paper to make templates. (Although you can reuse the freezer paper, it's better to have four paper horses so that you cut *on* the drawn line every time. You get a better edge that way.) Iron the freezer paper onto the black wool and cut out the horse on the drawn line. Carefully peel the paper off the wool, taking care not to distort the horse's skinny legs or tail.

2. Position a horse onto the center of a red 12½" wool square, centering it diagonally. Use a fabric-glue stick to baste the shape in place.

Finished quilt: 51" x 51"

Finished block: 12" x 12"

Repeat for a total of four blocks. Then appliqué the horses into place with the black pearl cotton or tapestry wool using a blanket stitch (page 91).

3. Draw a 6" square onto a sheet of the foundation paper. Copy this sheet 35 times on a photocopier for a total of 36 sheets. Trim the foundations to approximately 7" square (½" outside of the drawn line).

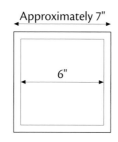
Approximately 7"
6"

4. Using your sewing machine, foundation piece the assorted neutral wool strips onto the square foundation. Begin by laying the first strip onto the paper diagonally from corner to corner with the "right" side up if one side of the wool is preferred. Position another strip on top of this strip with "right" sides together so that one edge of the top piece aligns with one edge of the bottom piece. Sew the pieces together, through the paper, ¼" from the aligned edges. When stitching these strips, use a small stitch so that the paper will easily tear away from the wool block.

5. Flip the top piece so that both strips are flat. Press. If they're in your way, trim the extra length from the wool strips. Continue adding strips in this manner, to each side of the center strip, until the entire foundation is covered. Repeat for the remaining 35 paper squares.

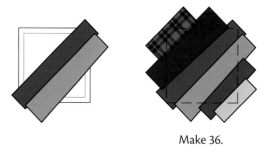

Make 36.

Save Time with Chain Piecing

When machine piecing the strip-pieced blocks, it is easier and faster to chain piece them. When you sew the second piece of wool to the first diagonal strip, continue this step on all 36 blocks. When this step is done, trim the threads in between each block and take all the blocks to the ironing board and press. Now all the blocks are ready for the third piece of wool to be sewn on. Continue in this manner until all the blocks are covered with strips.

6. Once all of the 36 blocks are done, carefully tear off the paper from the back of the blocks, taking care not to distort the stitches.

7. Using a rotary cutter, mat, and ruler, trim each square so that it is 6½" x 6½".

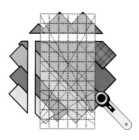

8. Sew two 6½" square blocks together as shown so that the angles form a V shape. Repeat to make 18 units. Press the seams open.

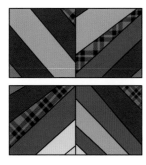

Make 18.

9. Sew the units from step 8 together in pairs to make nine blocks as shown. Press.

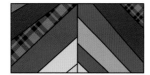

Make 9.

10. Arrange the pieced blocks, the horse blocks, and the red wool triangles in diagonal rows as shown. Sew the blocks and triangles into rows and press. Sew the rows together.

Embroidering the Details

Refer to "Embroidery Stitches" (page 91) to add stitched embellishments to the pieced blocks. You can stitch your initials or any wording you desire with a running stitch. Use feather stitches and blanket stitches to outline some of the pieces. You can even sew a spider's web, which was once considered good luck.

Finishing the Quilt

1. Cut the backing fabric in half to make two pieces, each approximately 58" long; sew the pieces together along this length. Trim to 55" square.

2. Center and layer the quilt top and batting over the backing; baste the layers together.

3. Quilt as desired using linen thread or quilting thread and an embroidery needle. The quilting motion is exactly the same as if you were using a smaller quilting needle; your stitches will simply be larger, allowing them to show up on the higher-loft wool fabric. This quilt was quilted in an allover fan pattern that I did not premark—it's easy once you try. If you are right-handed, start at the top or bottom right-hand corner and work your way to the left. Continue your rows in this manner. This more random quilting style adds to the primitive antique appearance.

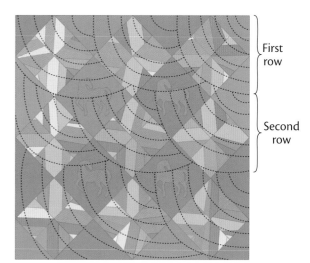

First row

Second row

4. This quilt was bound by bringing the backing fabric around to the front, in the manner of many antique wool quilts. Continue with these steps to do this, or refer to "Binding" (page 93) to bind in the traditional manner.

5. Trim the batting so that it is flush with the quilt top. Trim the backing so that it is 1" larger on all sides of the quilt.

6. Fold the backing under ½" and then turn the folded edge around to the front; sew down on the front side with a blind stitch.

7. Make a label and attach it to the back of your quilt.

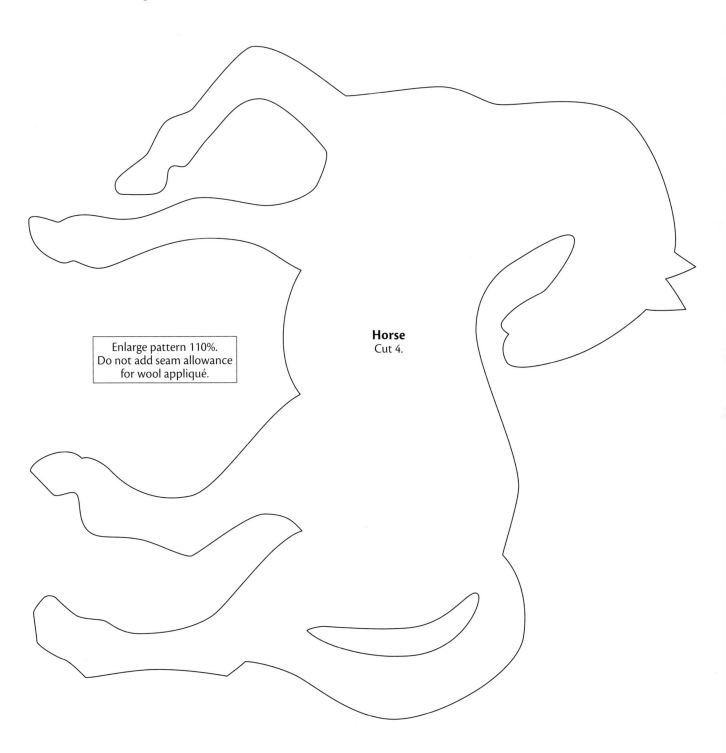

Enlarge pattern 110%.
Do not add seam allowance
for wool appliqué.

Horse
Cut 4.

Mornings on the Farm

This charming quilt is an exercise in improvisation. I think much of our quiltmaking is rigid and structured and can therefore be stifling to the creative spirit. This brightly colored quilt is my answer to that. Follow the directions as written, or feel free to make it your own.

Materials

Woven plaid fabrics are preferred for the barn. Fabrics for the entire quilt should be a combination of plaids, stripes, and prints.

1 yard of black plaid for barn roof, inner border, pieced border, and binding

⅞ yard of blue check for background and pieced border

⅝ yard of gold check for barn background and pieced border

½ yard of woven red check for barn boards and pieced border

½ yard of black print for rooster and pieced border

¼ yard *each* of 2 red striped fabrics for rooster, barn door, and pieced border

¼ yard *total* of assorted blue plaids and stripes for barn windows and pieced border

¼ yard *total* of assorted gold prints for rooster feet and pieced border

Scraps of black plaid for pieced border

1⅓ yards of fabric for backing

40" x 43" piece of batting

Washable fabric glue

Tear or Cut?

I suggest you tear your fabric to get the strips needed for the barn. If you cannot make yourself tear fabric, then by all means, cut it, but I find that tearing is useful and fun. First, it is easy and efficient. Second, your fabric is always on grain. Third, it feels like you're breaking the rules, which can free up your creativity.

When you tear the fabric for the barn, choose a woven plaid or striped fabric. A print may be used, but when the printed fabric is torn, the print design may distort up to ¼" from the edge. If you don't mind this distortion, a printed fabric can be used. A woven, yarn-dyed fabric will not distort in this way.

Finished quilt: 36" x 39"

Cutting

From the blue check, cut:

* 1 rectangle, 25" x 28"
* 12 rectangles, 1½" x 4½"

From the gold check, cut:

* 1 rectangle, 18" x 22"
* 10 rectangles, 1½" x 4½"

From the red check, cut:

* 13 rectangles, 1½" x 4½"
* Save the remaining fabric to tear (see "Tear or Cut?" on page 29).

From the red striped fabrics, cut:

* 1 square, 6" x 6", for the barn door*
* 1 comb piece (page 36)
* 1 neck feathers piece (page 37)
* 1 tail feathers piece (page 37)
* 22 rectangles, 1½" x 4½"

From the blue plaids and stripes, cut:

* 3 rectangles, 2" x 3½", for the barn windows*
* 22 rectangles, 1½" x 4½"

From the black plaid for barn roof, cut:

* 2 strips, 2½" x 28½"
* 2 strips, 2½" x 27"
* 9 rectangles, 1½" x 4½"
* 5 strips, 2¼" x 42"
* Save the remaining fabric to tear (see "Tear or Cut?" on page 29).

From the assorted gold prints, cut:

* 1 right foot piece (page 37)
* 1 left foot piece (page 37)
* 16 rectangles, 1½" x 4½"

From the black print, cut:

* 1 body piece (page 36)
* 1 wing piece (page 37)
* 11 rectangles, 1½" x 4½"

From the assorted black plaid scraps, cut:

* 5 rectangles, 1½" x 4½"

From the backing fabric, cut;

* 1 piece, 43" long by the width of the fabric

*These are approximate dimensions; there's no need for precise measurement. Cut the door and windows whatever size you like.

Making the Rooster and the Barn

1. The 18" x 22" gold check rectangle will create the height and width of your barn. If you want a smaller barn, trim the rectangle accordingly. The barn in the quilt shown is approximately 20" wide and 14" tall.

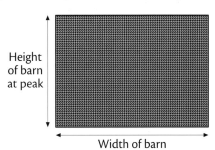

Height of barn at peak

Width of barn

2. Cut off the top right and left corners of the rectangle to create the barn shape. Improvise, and cut a shape that appeals to you.

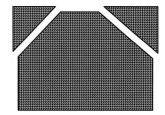

3. Place the gold barn fabric onto the 25" x 28" blue check rectangle, taking into consideration where you will place your rooster. With the right sides of both fabrics up, sew the gold barn fabric onto the background by machine stitching ⅛" from the raw edges of the gold check.

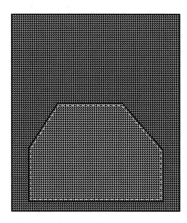

4. Turn this piece over and cut away the background behind the barn, leaving a ¼" seam allowance. Press.

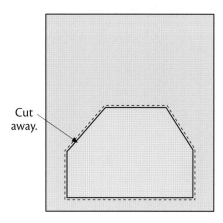

Cut away.

5. On the right side, arrange the door and windows on the barn. Once positioned, sew these in place ⅛" from the raw edges. Trim away the fabric from behind the doors and windows as you did for the barn.

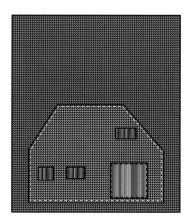

6. Tear the red check barn fabric into strips varying in width from 1" to 2". Don't measure, just tear by eye. These are the boards of the barn.

7. Lay down the first board on the side of the barn, covering the raw edge of the gold barn fabric. The top and bottom of your board should just meet the edge of the gold fabric. Cut to fit with scissors. These raw edges will be covered later.

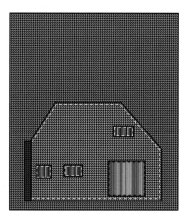

8. Appliqué the long edges of the board. You can appliqué leaving a raw edge or you can turn under the edge with the needle-turn-appliqué

technique. When the fabric is torn, the edge of the fabric does not necessarily turn under in a uniform way. It tends to act like bias. With the needle-turn-appliqué technique, the edges will be a little uneven and primitive looking.

9. Place a second strip next to the first. If you are using the needle-turn method, the edge should *just* overlap the preceding board. Once the appliqué edge is sewn down there will be a space for the gold fabric to show through. If you are doing raw-edge appliqué, leave a small gap so that the gold fabric will show through.

10. Continue adding boards in this manner until you have the side of the barn covered as shown. Remember to sew only the long ends; leave the short raw ends unsewn.

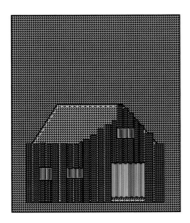

11. Now add boards to cover the raw edges above and below the windows and door. Appliqué a strip to the bottom edge of the barn, and then add a diagonal board to mimic a barn door.

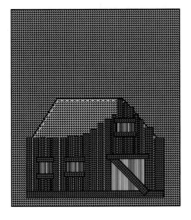

12. To make the roof, tear the black plaid fabric into approximately 2"-wide strips. Again, do not measure; just tear by eye. Place the first strip over the roof area along the bottom. Appliqué the bottom edge of the roof strip only. Leave the top edge free. Leave the short sides of the roof strips free as well. They will be covered later.

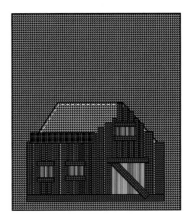

13. Appliqué the bottom edge of the next strip over the first strip and leave the top edge free. Continue adding roof boards in this manner until you are at the top of the barn.

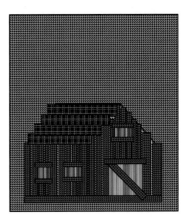

14. Appliqué three boards over the rooflines as shown to cover the raw edges of the barn and roof. Note that the top board is one long strip, slightly curved as you stitch it down.

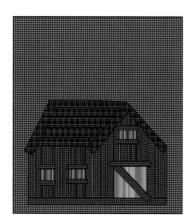

15. Appliqué the rooster in the following order: feet, comb, body, tail feathers, wing, and neck feathers.

16. Trim the quilt top to 24" x 27" and press using a pressing cloth.

Adding the Inner Border

Sew the two 2½" x 27" black plaid strips to the sides of the quilt top. Press the seam allowances toward the strips. Sew the 2½" x 28½" black plaid strips to the top and bottom of the quilt top. Press.

Making the Log Cabin Blocks

To make the corner Log Cabin blocks, cut the following pieces from leftover black plaid, black print, and blue plaid fabrics.

From the black fabrics, cut a total of:

 ✳ 4 squares, 1½" x 1½"

 ✳ 4 rectangles, 1½" x 2½"

 ✳ 4 rectangles, 1½" x 3½"

 ✳ 4 rectangles, 1½" x 4½"

From the blue fabrics, cut a total of:

 ✳ 4 squares, 1½" x 1½"

 ✳ 4 rectangles, 1½" x 2½"

 ✳ 4 rectangles, 1½" x 3½"

1. Sew black and blue 1½" squares together. Press the seam allowance toward the black square.

2. Sew a 2½" black rectangle to the right of this unit. Press the seam toward each newly added piece as you sew.

3. Add the 2½" blue piece, and then the 3½" blue piece.

4. Add the 3½" black strip next, and then the 4½" black strip. Repeat the steps to make four Log Cabin blocks.

Make 4.

Adding the Pieced Borders

1. Randomly place the assorted 1½" x 4½" rectangles together into four units. Two of these units should be made of 28 rectangles and two should be made of 32 rectangles.

2. Sew the rectangles together. The longer units should measure 31" long and the shorter units should measure 28" long. Trim the ends and take slightly wider seam allowances here and there to make the borders the correct length. This adds to the random nature of the quilt. Press the seam allowances in one direction.

3. Sew the 31" strips to the sides of the quilt top. Press the seam allowances toward the plaid border.

4. Sew a Log Cabin block to each end of the 28" top and bottom borders. Press the seam allowances toward the Log Cabin blocks and sew the borders to the top and bottom of the quilt. Press.

Finishing the Quilt

1. Choose a quilting design and then follow the directions for marking in "Marking the Quilt Top" (page 92).

2. Center and layer the quilt top and batting over the backing. Baste the layers together, and then quilt as desired. This quilt was hand quilted in an allover fan pattern using a large quilting stitch, which is a great way of hand quilting a top that has lots of seams and appliqué thicknesses.

3. Trim the batting and backing even with the edges of the quilt top. Use the 2¼" x 42" black plaid strips to bind the quilt referring to "Binding" (page 93).

4. Make a label and attach it to the back of your quilt.

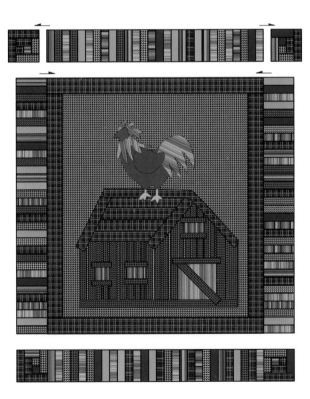

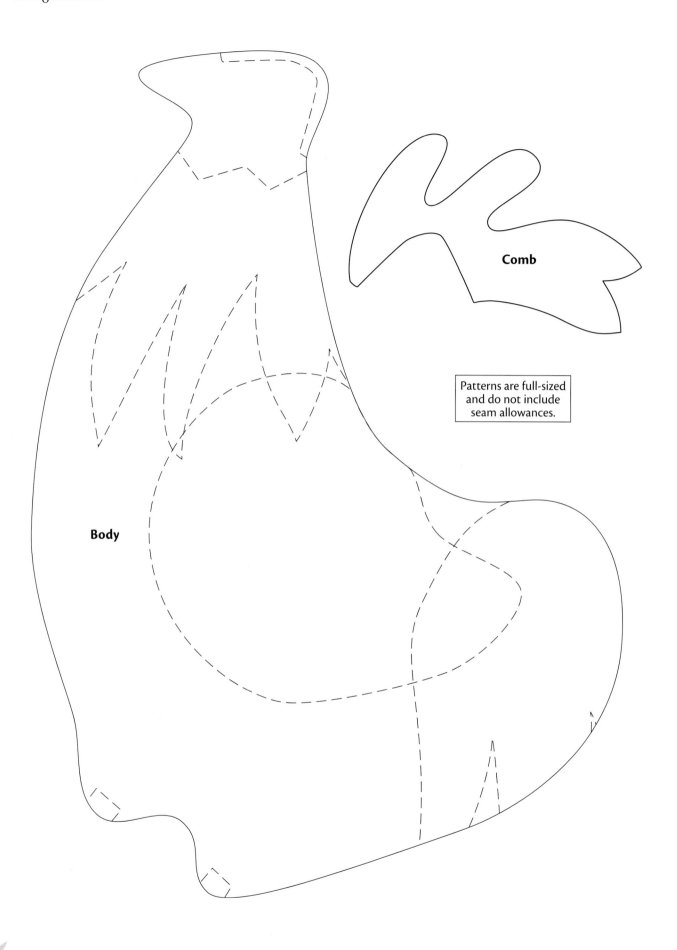

Comb

Patterns are full-sized
and do not include
seam allowances.

Body

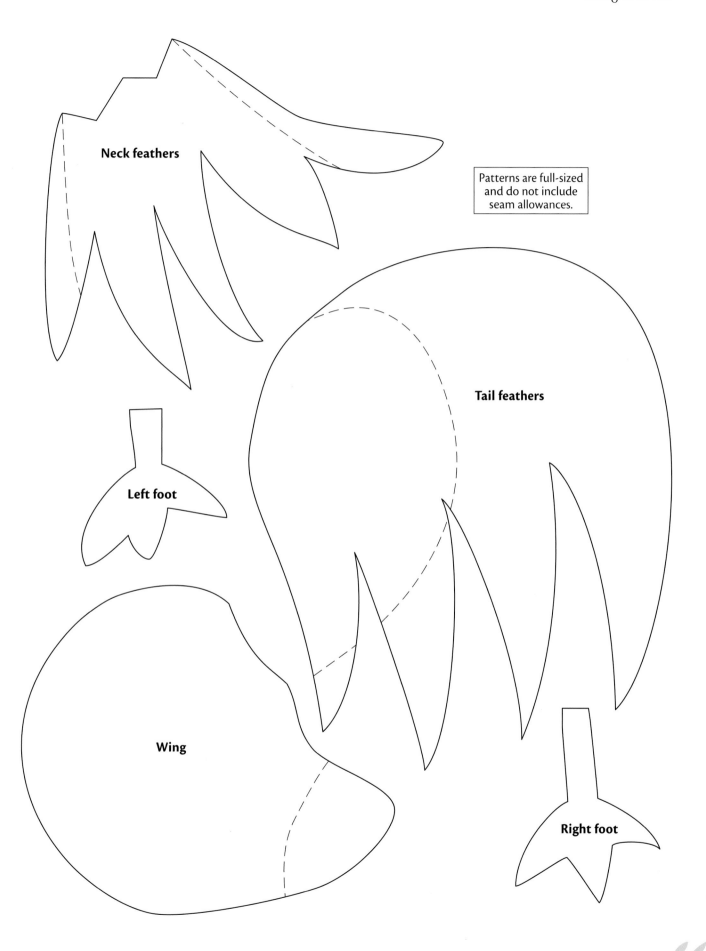

Neck feathers

Patterns are full-sized
and do not include
seam allowances.

Tail feathers

Left foot

Wing

Right foot

Prairie Cloth Bed Rug

My sister, Polly, and I collaborated on this project. She is a rug hooker, and antique bed rugs were often hooked. We thought a penny-rug style of bed covering would be fun to do and would use up many of our wool scraps. Polly hooked the vine border, but you can embroider it with wool tapestry yarn. We used prairie cloth, which is similar to homespun cotton, instead of wool as the background because it can be easily hooked through—and we like how it looks.

Materials

9½ yards of black prairie cloth*

5 yards *total* of assorted wool scraps
for pennies, flowers, and stars

8¾ yards of 42"-wide cotton fabric for backing

Black pearl cotton for appliqué and tying**

Wool tapestry yarn for embroidery

Chenille needle, size 20 or 22

This is for prairie cloth that is 54" wide. You will need 11⅞ yards if the prairie cloth is 42" wide.

**I used black Homestead 8/2 Cotton from Halcyon Yarn. The small 5" spool is plenty for this project.*

Cutting

Use the patterns (page 43) for the circles, but don't worry about making them perfectly round—some lopsided circles will add folk-art charm to your bed rug. Cut them by eye once you get a feel for it. There may be extra circles, depending on how many you use in the border areas.

From the assorted wool scraps, cut:
* 203 *each* of small, medium, and large circles

From the black prairie cloth, cut on the *lengthwise* grain:
* 2 pieces, 22" x 95"
* 2 pieces, 33" x 67"
* 1 piece, 22" x 65"
* 1 piece, 8" x 65"

From the backing fabric, cut:
* 2 pieces, 42" x 95"
* 1 piece, 25" x 95"

Cutting by Eye

I cut all the circles for the pennies by eye—without a template. I urge you to give it a try. It is fast, efficient, and your pennies will all be a little different, giving your bed rug a true folk-art look. If you must use a template, try this alternative: Make a template of your largest circle and trace onto about a dozen or so different pieces of wool. Trim this template just a bit (sometimes only taking a bit off one side to make it lopsided) and trace another dozen or so on assorted wool. Trim again and trace another dozen. Continue doing this until you have about 600 in sizes from large to small. Put three together and start sewing.

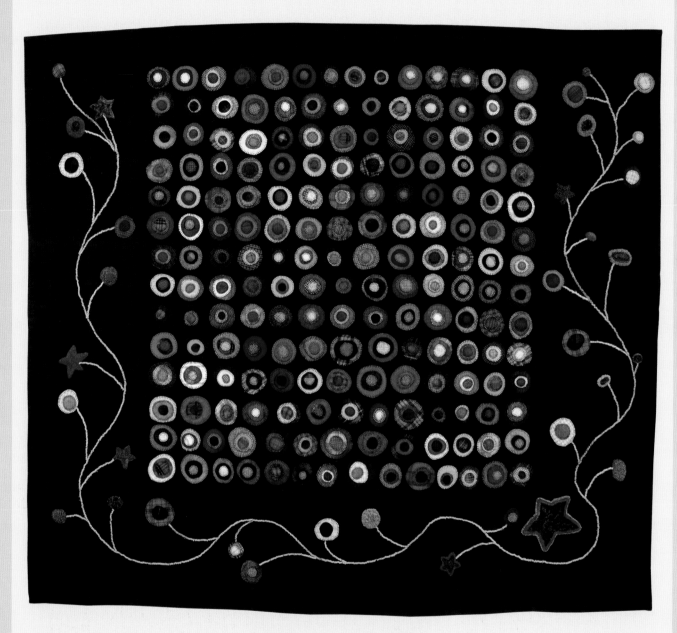

Finished bed rug: 103" x 91"

Assembling the Bed Rug

1. To make the pennies, sew 196 small circles to 196 medium circles using a blanket stitch. Reserve the remaining small and medium circles for the border.

2. Sew the units from step 1 onto 196 large circles using a blanket stitch. Reserve the remaining large circles for the border.

3. Sew the two 33" x 67" pieces of prairie cloth together with a ½" seam allowance so you have a finished piece that measures about 65" x 67". Press the seam allowances open. You may zigzag stitch or serge all around the outside edge to prevent fraying.

4. Arrange your pennies across this piece in 14 rows of 14 each until they are pleasing to you. Leave a 1" space all around each penny. If you look carefully at the photograph and count the pennies in each row, you'll see that not all the rows have 14 pennies. This adds to the folk-art charm. The instructions and cutting are written for 14 rows of 14 pennies each, but don't worry if you don't have space for all the pennies.

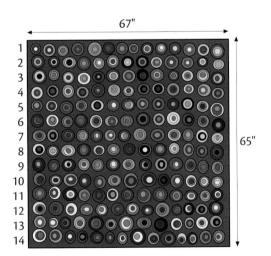

5. Remove row 14, stacking the pennies in order so that the penny on the left is on top of the stack, and safety pin the stack together. Label the stack as row 14.

6. Do this for rows 13 through row 2, pinning and labeling each stack.

7. Using a fabric-glue stick, glue the 14 pennies of row 1 to the prairie cloth. Blanket-stitch them all in place.

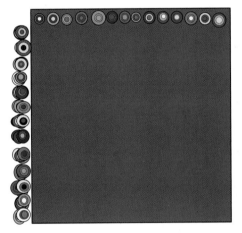

8. Remove the top penny of each of your pinned stacks and adhere each one with fabric glue into position on the left edge of the prairie cloth. Keep the remaining pennies stacked, pinned, and labeled.

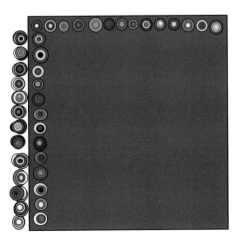

9. Stitch these pennies to the prairie cloth with a blanket stitch. Once these pennies are in place the next rows will be easier to place, by eye, in their respective positions. Place the second penny of rows 2–14 in position and adhere with fabric glue. Blanket-stitch in place.

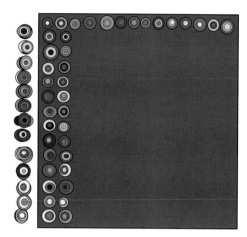

10. Continue adding pennies in this manner until all the pennies are blanket-stitched into place.

11. Sew the 8" x 65" piece to the top of the bed rug and the 22" x 65" piece to the bottom using a ½" seam allowance. Press the seam allowances open.

12. Sew the 22" x 95" pieces to the sides of this section. Press the seam allowances open.

Adding the Border

1. Lay your bed rug out flat on the floor and use a chalk pencil or a silver fabric pencil to draw a curving, meandering line around the two sides and bottom of the bed rug. Remember, this is *folk art*—you don't want the line to be perfectly balanced or symmetrical, so don't fret.

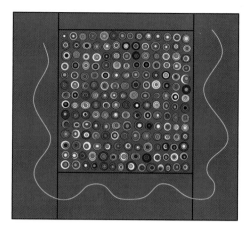

2. Draw a few offshoots on the vine. These offshoots should lead to an open area where a wool star or penny can be placed. Polly made 31 offshoots, but you can make fewer or more as you desire.

3. Embroider your vine using tapestry yarn, the chenille needle, and a chain stitch. Refer to "Embroidery Stitches" (page 91). If you prefer, hook the vine using #8 (¼"-wide) strips of wool.

4. Once the vine is done, cut and appliqué (or hook) assorted-wool pennies and stars to the ends of each vine. It's up to you if you want to add stars, two-layer pennies, or three-layer pennies to each vine offshoot. You could even add flower or heart shapes. Polly also added a larger star to the bottom right of the bed rug.

Tying the Layers

1. Piece the backing fabric panels together as shown and press the seam allowances open.

2. Lay the bed-rug top, right side down, on a flat surface. Layer the backing over this, right side up, and pin baste the layers together. There is no batting.

3. Using black pearl cotton and a chenille needle, tie the bed rug between each penny in the center section. Work from the backing side and take care, by feel, to insert the needle through only the backing and the prairie cloth. Bring the needle point back through to the backing, making a stitch on the front. Do not stitch through the pennies. Cut the thread and tie a square knot on the back of the bed rug. Trim the ends of the ties to approximately 1" long. The almost-invisible stitch is all that shows on the quilt front.

4. Continue tying in this manner into the border, placing a tie approximately every 5". Again, take care to only tie through the backing and prairie cloth, not the wool shapes.

5. To finish the edges, turn the edges of both the top and backing under 1" and press. Turn under 1" again and sew together using a blind stitch.

6. Make a label and attach it to the back of your bed rug.

Tying in a Floor Frame

If you have access to a large floor quilting frame, that is the easiest way to tie this bed rug. I put my top and backing in upside down so I could tie on the back of the bed rug. I used the same black pearl cotton I used to blanket-stitch and put a tie between each penny in the center section.

I began on the back side of the bed rug with a very long piece of pearl cotton. I took a stitch, moved over 5" to 6", and took another stitch. I did this by feel so as not to tie through the circles and continued across in a row until I reached the left side of the bed rug. I did not cut the thread in between. It looked like one small stitch and a very long stitch (5" to 6") all the way across. Then I clipped halfway between each small stitch so that I had a small stitch with two tails. I tied the tails into a square knot and then trimmed the tails to 1". In the border I put in a tie approximately every 5" or so, taking care not to tie through the vine or the flowers.

Patterns are full-sized.
Do not add seam allowances for wool appliqué.

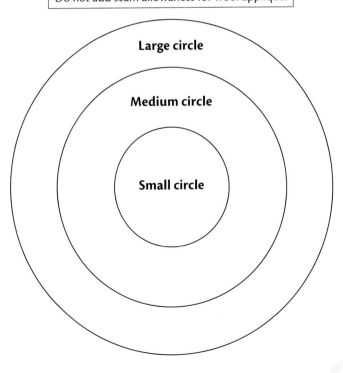

Large circle

Medium circle

Small circle

Old-Time Halloween Quilt

This quilt was inspired by a quilt that I saw at an antique show. Based on the fabrics used in the original, it appeared to be made in the 1920s. It was well used, worn, and faded. I loved how the black fabrics had washed out into many different dark shades—a look I tried to capture when I made this quilt. If you look closely, many of the "black" fabrics are not black at all, but khaki, gray, olive, or brown. I imagined that they all could have been black at one time, but time and wear had taken their toll.

Materials

All yardages are based on 42"-wide fabric.

8 yards *total* of assorted black and dark fabrics for blocks, border, and binding

5 yards *total* of assorted orange fabrics for blocks

8 yards of fabric for backing

86" x 104" piece of batting

1 skein *each* of ecru, gray, and charcoal pearl cotton

Cutting

From the black and dark fabrics, cut:

* 48 squares, 4½" x 4½"
* 54 strips, 1½" x 5½"
* 54 strips, 1½" x 6½"
* 54 strips, 1½" x 7½"
* 54 strips, 1½" x 8½"
* 54 strips, 1½" x 9½"
* 54 strips, 1½" x 10½"
* 54 strips, 1½" x 11½"
* 54 strips, 1½" x 12½"
* 64 squares, 4" x 4"; cut each square once diagonally to make 128 triangles
* 10 strips, 2¼" x 42", for binding

From the orange fabrics, cut:

* 48 strips, 1½" x 4½"
* 48 strips, 1½" x 5½"
* 48 strips, 1½" x 6½"
* 48 strips, 1½" x 7½"
* 48 strips, 1½" x 8½"
* 48 strips, 1½" x 9½"
* 48 strips, 1½" x 10½"
* 48 strips, 1½" x 11½"

Finished quilt: 80" x 98"

Finished block: 12"

Making the Log Cabin Blocks

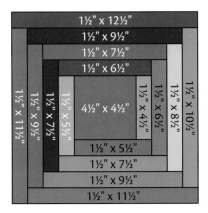

1½" x 12½"
1½" x 9½"
1½" x 7½"
1½" x 6½"
1½" x 11½"
1½" x 9½"
1½" x 7½"
1½" x 5½"
4½" x 4½"
1½" x 4½"
1½" x 6½"
1½" x 8½"
1½" x 10½"
1½" x 5½"
1½" x 7½"
1½" x 9½"
1½" x 11½"

1. Sew the 1½" x 4½" orange strips to the 4½" black squares. Press the seam allowances toward the orange fabric.

Chain Sewing

When making the Log Cabin blocks, it is most efficient to repeat each step 48 times, cut apart and press, and then go on to the next step. For example, chain piece a 4½" black square to a 1½" x 4½" orange strip 48 times. Snip these segments apart and press. Then move to step 2, adding the 1½" x 5½" orange strips to each of the units. Continue in this manner to make all 48 Log Cabin blocks at once. If you get confused as to which side of your unit the next strip should go on, here's a handy reminder: always add the strip to the side of the block that has the most seams. You might want to put all the pieces of the same color and size into stacks, and then lay them out in the formation of the finished Log Cabin block.

2. Sew the 1½" x 5½" orange strips to the units. Press the seam allowances toward the newly added strips. As new rounds are sewn, always press the seam allowances in the direction of the piece just added.

3. Sew the 5½" black strips to the units. Press. Turn the units a quarter turn and add the 6½" black strips to the next side.

4. Sew the 6½" orange strips to the units, followed by the 7½" orange strips. Continue adding the strips in the same manner, with orange strips on two adjacent sides of the units and black strips on the other two sides until the final two black strips are added. Each block should have eight orange strips and nine black pieces and should measure 12½" x 12½".

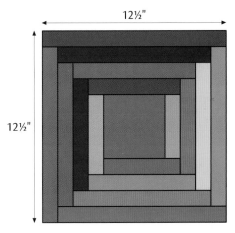

12½"

12½"

Make 48.

5. Embroider some of the blocks with cats, pumpkins, and the word *Halloween* using an outline stitch. You'll find cat and pumpkin patterns on page 50. Note that the *Halloween* letters need to be in adjacent blocks that are oriented correctly.

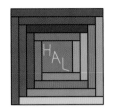

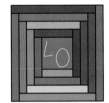
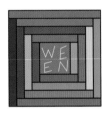

6. Lay out the blocks in eight rows of six blocks each as shown. Sew the blocks together in rows. Press in opposite directions from row to row. Sew the rows together. Press.

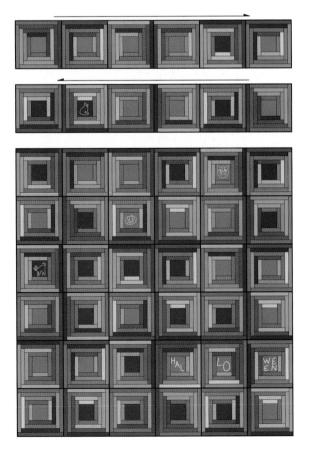

Making the Border

1. Sew the black 4" triangles together to make 64 triangle squares. Press the seam allowances to one side.

Make 64.

2. Stitch the squares together to make two strips of 32 squares each. Press the seam allowances in one direction.

Make 2.

3. Place a strip on each side of your quilt top. Trim the strips so that they are the exact length of your quilt top. Sew the strips to each side of your quilt. Press the seam allowances toward the center.

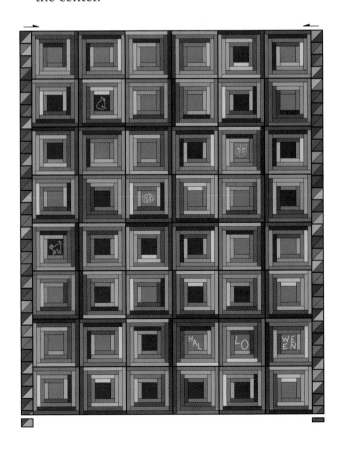

4. Piece the leftover 1½"-wide black strips into four long strips, making sure two are at least 81" long and the other two are at least 100" long.

5. Measure your quilt top through the center vertically and cut the two long pieces this length. Sew these to the sides of your quilt. Press the seam allowances toward the strips.

6. Measure your top through the center horizontally and cut the remaining strips to the width of your quilt top. Sew these to the top and bottom of your quilt. Press the seam allowances toward the strips.

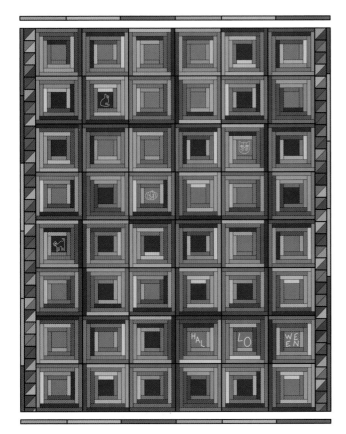

Finishing the Quilt

1. Choose a quilting design and follow the directions for marking in "Marking the Quilt Top" (page 92).

2. From the backing fabric, cut two pieces, 41" x 86", and one piece, 24" x 86". Join the pieces along their long edges to make a backing that's 86" x 104". Press the seam allowances open.

3. Center and layer the quilt top and batting over the backing; baste the layers together, and then quilt as desired. The quilt shown was quilted in an allover fan pattern drawn free-form and quilted with a big stitch.

4. Trim the batting and backing even with the edges of the quilt top. Use the 2¼" x 42" black strips to bind the quilt, referring to "Binding" (page 93).

5. Make and attach a label to the back of your quilt.

Easy Hand Quilting

The quilting on this quilt was fun and very fast. I used a wool batting, which is a great choice for any hand quilting, but is especially helpful to use with a top that has many seams. You may think that wool batting would be thick and bulky, but when hand quilted, it compresses to almost negligible bulk and it is a dream to needle. I used a big stitch to give it a primitive look, and this also speeded up the process. Lastly, I marked this top with a Hera marker after it was basted. I did a freehand fan design, marking one set of concentric arcs at a time. Many antique quilts were quilted freehand, and I like the look.

Patterns are full-sized.

Hooked Pillow Topper

Once again I collaborated with my sister, Polly, to make a unique pillow (or table) topper. You can make a similar piece with a hooked center as shown here, or you could appliqué the word *Halloween* on a piece of black wool. Adapt the cat embroidery patterns to create hooked designs or wool appliqués. The hooked rug in the center is approximately 35" x 6½", plus ½" binding all around. The center is surrounded by four layers of tongues (pattern at right).

To make the backing and tongues for the pillow topper, you'll need:

- ½ yard of black felt, at least 44" wide, for backing
- 1 yard of charcoal gray wool, at least 54" wide, for tongues

1. Hook or appliqué the center section to create an oval that is approximately 35½" x 7". If it is a hooked piece, bind the edges to finish them. If it is wool appliqué, an edge finish is not needed.
2. Cut an oval piece of felt 44" x 16", which is 1" smaller (all the way around) than the final size of the piece.
3. Cut 166 tongues from the charcoal gray wool and blanket-stitch around the curved edges.
4. Attach an outer bottom round of tongues (46 total) to the outside edge of the felt oval,

overlapping the tongues by about ½" and letting them overhang the oval by 1". Use a whipstitch or running stitch and a heavier thread such as quilting thread or pearl cotton.

5. Stitch the next round of tongues on top of the first round, letting the original round show underneath by 1" or so. Continue adding tongues until you've attached four rounds.
6. Center the bound hooked rug (or appliqué piece) on top of the felt oval and use safety pins to hold it in place. Stitch the rug to the felt with an up-and-down stab stitch (through all the layers) between the hooking and the binding.

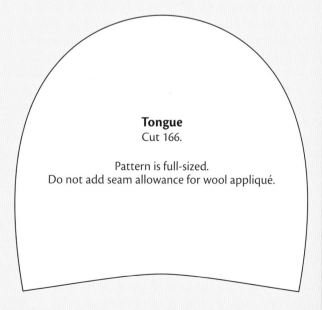

Tongue
Cut 166.

Pattern is full-sized.
Do not add seam allowance for wool appliqué.

Fiesta Quilt

I made this quilt to hang in my dining room to accompany my vintage Fiesta dinnerware. This quilt is kind of a strange hybrid of bright, Art Deco colors toned down with soft neutrals. This combination let me keep the bright colors, but softened it enough so the quilt could be lived with every day. Try mixing your bright fabrics with soft neutrals and see how they can complement each other.

Materials

All yardages are based on 42"-wide fabric.

5½ yards of dark plaid for background, border, and binding

2½ yards *total* of assorted teal prints and stripes for appliqués

1⅝ yards of medium neutral fabric for sashing

1⅝ yards *total* of assorted red prints and stripes for appliqués

½ yard *total* of assorted yellow stripes for appliqués

6" x 6" piece of beige print for appliqués

5½" yards of fabric for backing

78" x 92" piece of batting

Washable fabric glue

½" bias-tape maker (optional; see page 88)

Cutting

From the dark plaid, cut:

* 4 blocks, 22" x 29"

* 2 pieces, 9½" x 68½", from the lengthwise grain

* 2 pieces, 9½" x 72½", from the lengthwise grain

* 9 strips, 2¼" x 42"

From the medium neutral sashing fabric, cut:

* 2 strips, 4½" x 28½", from the lengthwise grain

* 3 strips, 4½" x 46½", from the lengthwise grain

* 4 strips, 4½" x 34½"

From the teal prints and stripes, cut:

* 1" bias strips to total 16½ yards.
This does not have to be continuous. The longest strips, used in the side borders, need to be approximately 44" in length.

Cutting the Appliqués

Use the patterns on pages 58–63. For the circles, make templates or cut freehand. Make ½" bias tape from all the bias stem pieces.

For *each* block, cut the following appliqué pieces:

* 1 red rectangle, 13" x 15", for the pitcher

* 1 contrasting red rectangle, 7" x 8", for the pitcher's reverse-appliqué highlights

* 1 red rectangle, 3" x 4", for the reverse-appliqué veins of leaf L

Continued on page 55

Finished quilt: 72" x 86"

Finished block: 21" x 28"

Continued from page 53

✳ 2 to 4 red circles

✳ 1 red J piece

✳ 1 red K piece

✳ 1 teal bias stem from the darker bias strips: 10¾" long for stem A

✳ 3 teal bias stems from the bias strips: 10" long for stem B, 16½" long for stem C, and 17" long for stem D

✳ 1 teal E piece

✳ 1 teal F piece

✳ 1 teal G piece

✳ 1 teal I piece

✳ 1 teal rectangle, 5" x 9", for leaf L

✳ 1 teal M piece and 1 teal M reversed piece

✳ 1 yellow H piece

✳ 10 to 12 yellow circles

✳ 1 beige circle

For the border, cut:

✳ 2 red urns

✳ 2 red teacups

✳ 4 red J pieces

✳ 4 red K pieces

✳ 4 red P pieces

✳ 4 red Q pieces

✳ 8 teal I pieces

✳ 4 teal J pieces

✳ 4 teal K pieces

✳ 4 teal N pieces

✳ 4 teal O pieces

✳ 36 to 40 red circles of varying sizes

✳ 16 to 24 yellow circles of varying sizes

✳ Approximately 380" of teal bias stems using the bias strips

Making the Blocks

1. Mark the pitcher pattern on the 13" x 15" red rectangle. Baste the 7" x 8" contrasting red square to the back of the fabric. The right sides of both fabrics should be facing up.

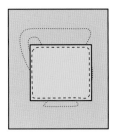 

2. Reverse appliqué the curved pitcher highlight lines so that the background fabric shows through. Trim away the excess red background fabric. Refer to "Reverse Appliqué" on page 90.

3. Repeat the reverse-appliqué technique for the large teal L leaf using the 5" x 9" teal rectangle with the 3" x 4" red piece behind it.

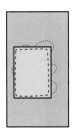  

4. Cut out the pitcher and leaf shapes so that they both have a ⅛" seam allowance.

5. Appliqué the pieces to the dark plaid background in the following order: bias stems A,

B, C, and D; E, F, G, H, I, J, K, L, M and M reversed; pitcher; and circles.

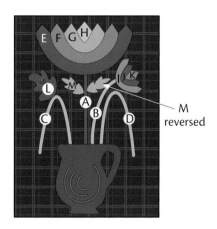

6. Repeat for the other three blocks. Press. Trim the blocks to 21½" x 28½".

7. Sew a 4½" x 28½" sashing piece between each set of two blocks. Press the seam allowances toward the sashing.

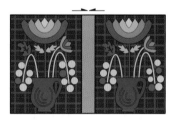

8. Sew the three 4½" x 46½" sashing pieces and the two block rows together. Press the seam allowances toward the sashing.

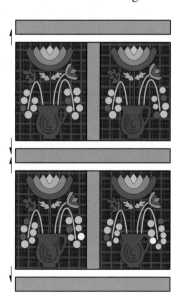

9. Sew two 4½" x 34½" sashing strips together to make a 4½" x 68½" strip. Press the seam allowance to one side. Make two. Sew these strips to the sides of the blocks. Press the seam allowances toward the sashing.

10. Sew the two 9½" x 68½" dark plaid strips to the sides of the quilt top. Press the seam allowances toward the dark plaid.

11. Sew the two 9½" x 72½" dark plaid strips to the top and bottom of the quilt top. Press the seam allowances toward the dark plaid.

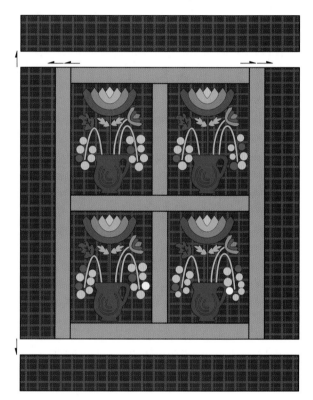

Appliquéing the Border

Appliqué the border pieces into place referring to the diagram on page 57 and the photograph (page 54). I marked and appliquéd all the bias stems first; I did it freehand. Draw the vine lines onto the fabric and run a bead of Roxanne's Glue-Baste-It or other washable fabric glue along one stem line.

56

Glue and appliqué one length of bias at a time. Lay the bias stem on top of the line of glue and press with a hot iron. You do not need much glue. Continue appliquéing the stems in this manner. Then appliqué the containers and flowers on top. Appliqué the flower petals in alphabetical order as you did for the blocks.

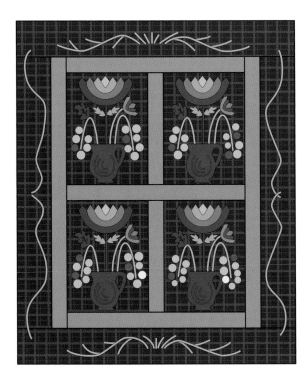

Finishing the Quilt

1. Choose a quilting design, and then mark as necessary. Follow the directions in "Marking the Quilt Top" (page 92). This quilt was marked after it was basted and as I went. There is outline quilting around the pitchers and the flowers and vines. I added some curving lines inside some of the larger flower shapes. The backgrounds of the four blocks were quilted in a crosshatch pattern that I marked with 1"-wide masking tape. The sashing was quilted in a cable design. In the border there is more outline quilting around the vines and flowers; these shapes were echo quilted into the background and were not marked. The only chalk or pencil marking on the quilt was in the sashing and the curving lines in the large flower shapes.

2. From the backing fabric, cut two 94" lengths. Sew them together so that you have a piece that is approximately 80" x 94". Press the seam allowance open.

3. Center and layer the quilt top and batting over the backing; baste the layers together and quilt as desired.

4. Trim the batting and backing even with the edges of the quilt top. Use the 2¼" x 42" dark plaid strips to bind the quilt referring to "Binding" (page 93).

5. Make and attach a label to the back of your quilt.

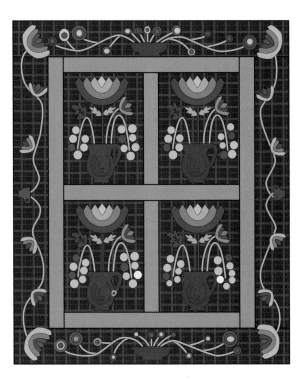

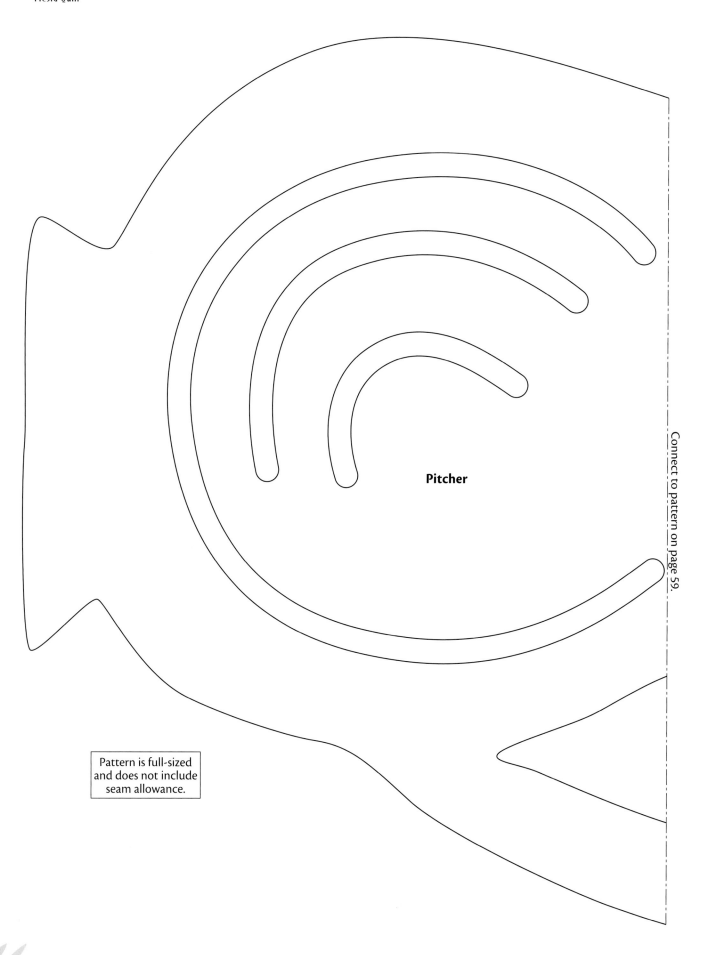

Pitcher

Connect to pattern on page 59.

Pattern is full-sized
and does not include
seam allowance.

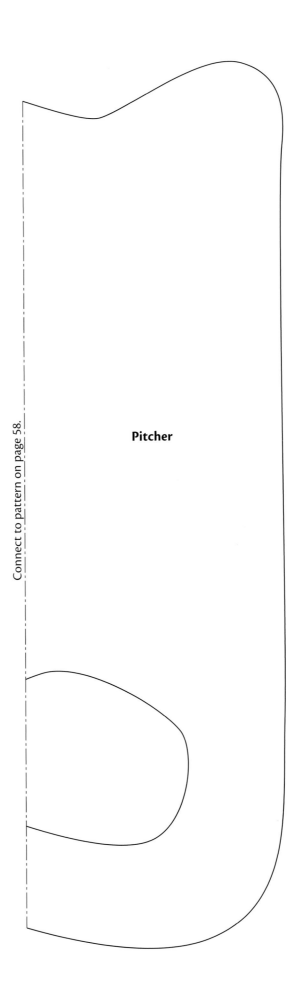

Pitcher

Connect to pattern on page 58.

Pattern is full-sized and does not include seam allowance.

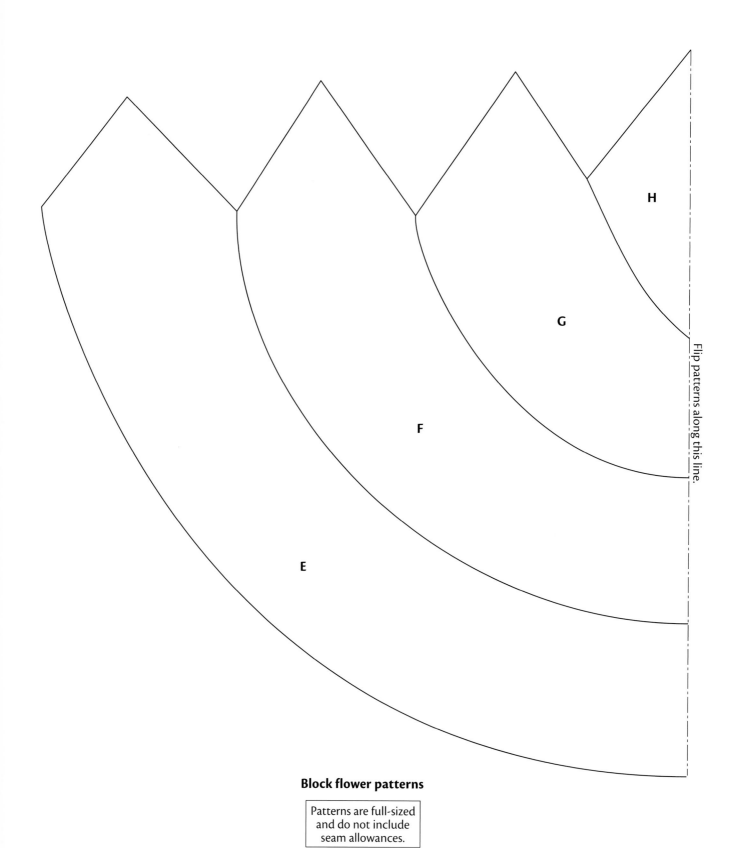

H

G

F

E

Flip patterns along this line.

Block flower patterns

Patterns are full-sized
and do not include
seam allowances.

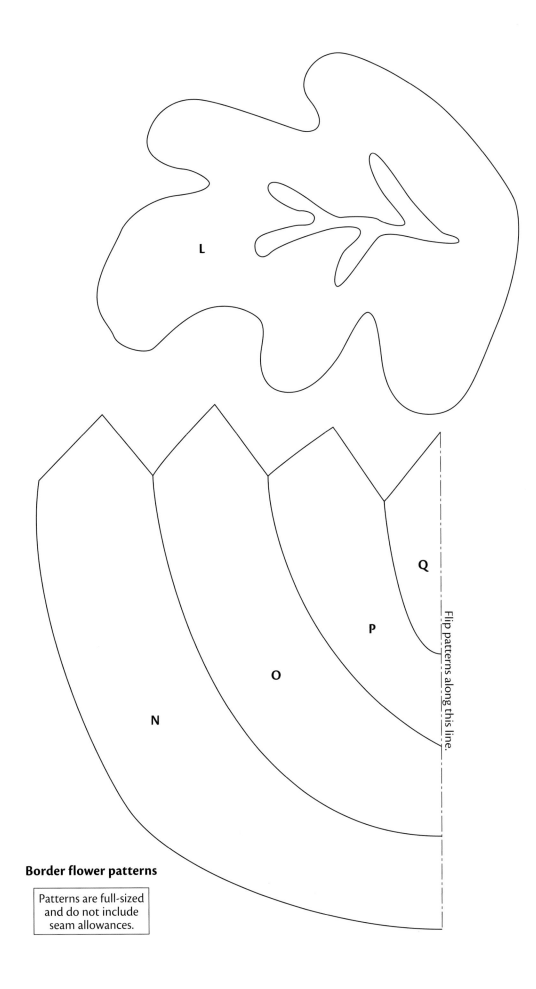

L

Q

P

O

N

Flip patterns along this line.

Border flower patterns

Patterns are full-sized
and do not include
seam allowances.

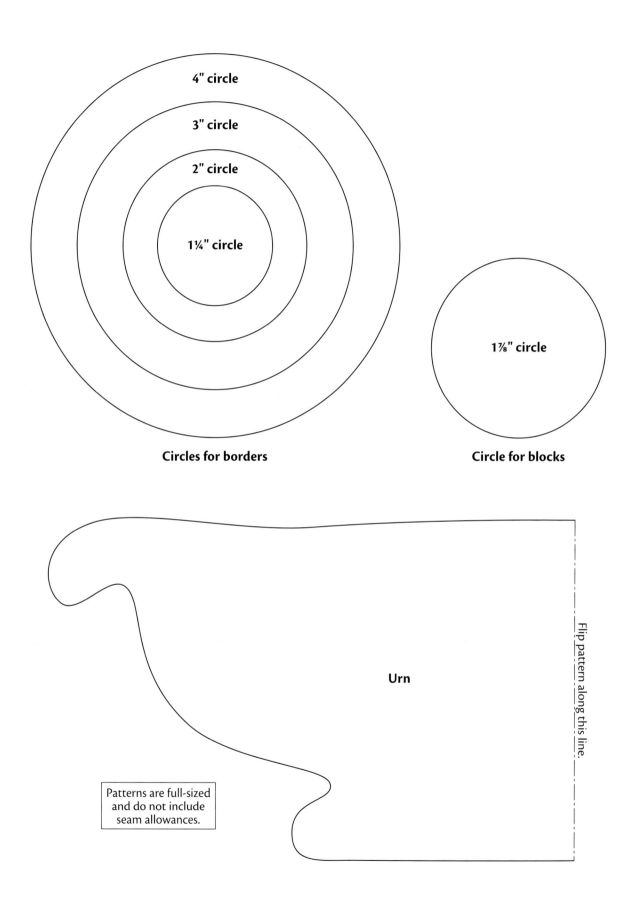

4" circle

3" circle

2" circle

1¼" circle

Circles for borders

1⅞" circle

Circle for blocks

Urn

Flip pattern along this line.

Patterns are full-sized
and do not include
seam allowances.

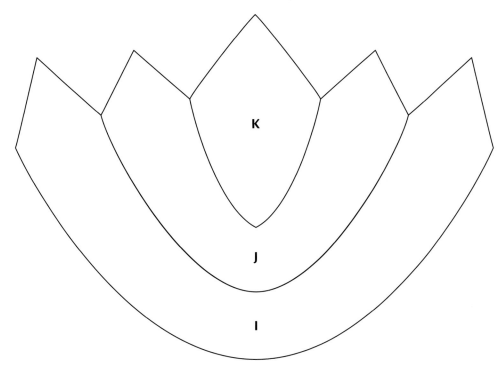

Block and border flower patterns

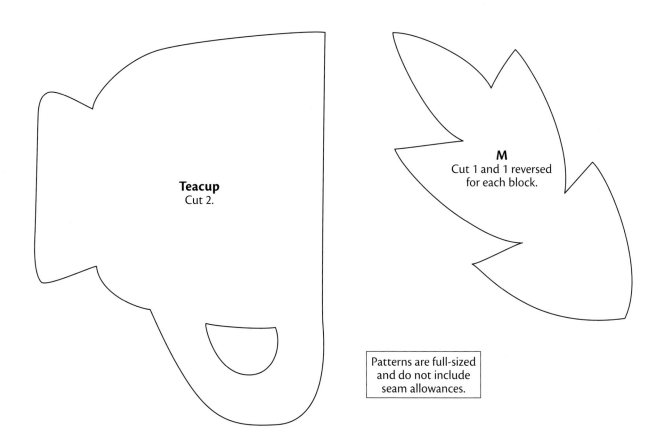

Teacup
Cut 2.

M
Cut 1 and 1 reversed
for each block.

Patterns are full-sized
and do not include
seam allowances.

Japanese Baskets

A bundle of Japanese quilting fabric in soft, neutral shades was the starting point for this quilt. I love the subtle textures and the complex, layer-upon-layer design in these textiles. When you use limited color, you must rely on value to make your design. This quilt is a favorite of mine.

Materials

¼ yard *each* or scraps of 24 assorted light, medium, and dark neutrals for Basket blocks and pieced border

1⅝ yards of neutral plaid for pieced border and binding

⅝ yard of dark neutral #1 for plain blocks and corner setting triangles

½ yard of dark neutral #2 for side setting triangles

¼ yard of dark neutral #3 for corner setting triangles

3 yards of fabric for backing

48" x 59" piece of batting

Choosing Values

Use a range of neutral fabrics from light to dark, with most in the medium-dark to dark range.

Cutting

Since the blocks are scrappy, cutting is given for one block. Repeat the cutting for all 12 blocks.

Cutting for One Basket Block

From the basket background fabric, cut:

✳ 2 A strips, 2" x 5"

✳ 1 B square, 5⅜" x 5⅜"; cut once diagonally to make 2 triangles. 1 is extra.

✳ 3 C squares, 2⅜" x 2⅜"; cut each square once diagonally to make 6 triangles

✳ 1 D square, 3⅞" x 3⅞"; cut once diagonally to make 2 triangles. 1 is extra.

✳ 1 E square, 2" x 2"

From the basket fabric, cut:

✳ 1 B square, 5⅜" x 5⅜"; cut once diagonally to make 2 triangles. 1 is extra.

✳ 4 C squares, 2⅜" x 2⅜"; cut each square once diagonally to make 8 triangles

Cutting for the Remainder of the Quilt

From dark neutral #1, cut:

✳ 6 squares, 8" x 8"

✳ 1 square, 6¼" x 6¼"; cut once diagonally to make 2 triangles

Continued on page 67

Finished quilt: 42" x 52½"

Finished block: 7½" x 7½"

Continued from page 65

From dark neutral #2, cut:

✳ 3 squares, 1⅞" x 1⅞"; cut each square twice diagonally to make 12 triangles. 2 are extra.

From dark neutral #3, cut:

✳ 1 square, 6¼" x 6¼"; cut once diagonally to make 2 triangles

From the neutral plaid, cut on the *lengthwise* grain:

✳ 2 strips, 2½" x 43"

✳ 2 strips, 2½" x 36½"

✳ 4 strips, 1½" x 42"

✳ 2 strips, 2½" x 49"

✳ 2 strips, 2½" x 41½"

✳ 4 strips, 2¼" x 50", for binding

✳ 21 squares, 1⅞" x 1⅞"; cut each square once diagonally to make 42 triangles

From the remaining assorted light neutrals, cut:

✳ 21 squares, 1⅞" x 1⅞"; cut each square once diagonally to make 42 triangles

Making the Basket Blocks

The directions are written to make one block at a time.

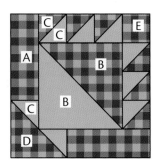

1. Sew a C triangle cut from basket fabric to a C triangle cut from background fabric to make a triangle-square unit. Make six. Press the seam allowances toward the darker fabric.

Make 6.

2. Sew a background B triangle to a basket B triangle. Press the seam allowances toward the darker fabric.

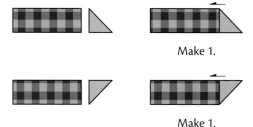

Make 1.

3. Sew a C basket triangle to the end of an A background piece as shown. Press. Make a second unit with the triangle facing the opposite direction.

Make 1.

Make 1.

4. Sew three triangle-square units from step 1 together as shown. Press. Make a second unit with the triangles facing the opposite direction.

Make 1.

Make 1.

5. Sew the E basket square to one end of a unit from step 4. Sew this and the remaining unit from step 4 to the B triangle square, taking care to orient the basket triangles as shown. Press the seam allowances toward the B triangle square.

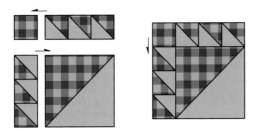

6. Add the two units from step 3. Press the seam allowances to the just-added units.

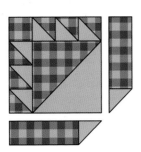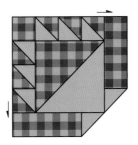

7. Sew the D background triangle to the block. Press the seam allowance toward the D piece. Repeat steps 1 through 7 to make 12 blocks.

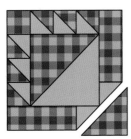

Make 12.

Assembling the Quilt Top

Arrange the Basket blocks, plain blocks, and the setting triangles together as shown. Sew the blocks and side triangles into diagonal rows. Press toward the setting squares and triangles. Sew the rows together and add the corner triangles last. Press.

Assembling the Border

1. Sew the two 2½" x 43" neutral plaid pieces to the sides of the quilt top. Press.

2. Sew the two 2½" x 36½" neutral plaid pieces to the top and bottom. Press.

3. Sew the 1⅞" neutral plaid and assorted light neutral triangles together to make 42 triangle-square units. Referring to the quilt photograph (page 66), arrange these around the quilt until you are pleased with the layout. Cut and sew additional triangle squares if desired, or use fewer if you prefer.

4. Sew the triangle-square units together. Cut the 1½" x 42" neutral plaid strips as needed and sew them to the pieced triangle-square units as shown. Press toward the unpieced strips. Place these strips along the top, bottom, and sides of your quilt top in a design that is pleasing to you.

5. When you're happy with the layout, trim the two side pieces so that they measure 1½" x 47½". Sew them to the sides of your quilt top. Press the seam allowances toward the inside.

6. Trim the top and bottom pieces so that they measure 1½" x 38½". Sew them to the top and bottom of your quilt top. Press.

Trim excess.

7. Sew the 2½" x 49" neutral plaid pieces to the sides of your quilt top. Press.

8. Sew the 2½" x 41½" neutral plaid pieces to the top and bottom of your quilt top. Press.

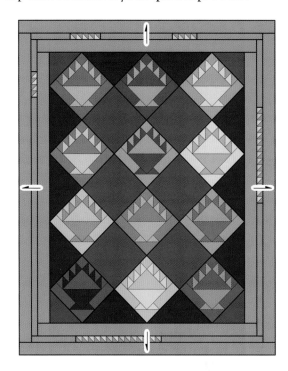

Finishing the Quilt

1. Cut the backing fabric into pieces measuring 50" x 42" and 50" x 20". Sew the two pieces together along the 50" length and press the seam allowances open.

2. Choose a quilting design and then follow the directions for marking in "Marking the Quilt Top" (page 92).

3. Center and layer the quilt top and batting over the backing; baste the layers together and quilt as desired. This quilt was quilted in an allover fan pattern—a favorite of mine as you can see!

4. Trim the batting and backing even with the quilt top. Use the 2¼" x 50" neutral plaid strips to bind the quilt referring to "Binding" (page 93).

5. Make and attach a label to the back of your quilt.

Wool Stars Quilt

3. Set your sewing machine to a long stitch length and sew the prairie points into place along the raw edge of the quilt top using a ¼" seam allowance. The tips of the triangles should remain unattached.

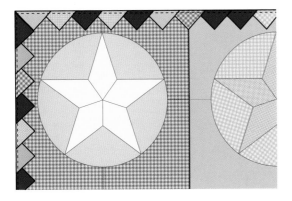

Finishing the Quilt

1. Center the quilt top over the backing and baste the two layers together. I don't recommend using a basting spray on this two-layer wool quilt because the wool is very porous. It would absorb the adhesive and would not stick together very well.

2. Quilt as desired using cotton quilting thread or a heavier linen thread. When hand quilting wool, use a big stitch and a long needle. I used an embroidery needle. The quilting motion is exactly the same as regular quilting with a smaller needle; your stitches will simply be larger, allowing them to show on the wool. Move the prairie points out of your way as you quilt near them. Leave a ½" margin unquilted all the way around the perimeter of your quilt.

3. Trim the backing so that it is ½" larger all around the quilt top.

4. Fold the prairie points up and away from the center of the quilt. Turn under their long raw edges. Turn under the raw edge of the quilt backing toward the inside of the quilt and pin.

5. Working from the back, stitch the backing edge to the quilt-top edge with yarn or pearl cotton using a blanket stitch or whipstitch. This will encase the raw edges of the prairie points and finish the edges of the quilt.

6. Make and attach a label to the back of your quilt.

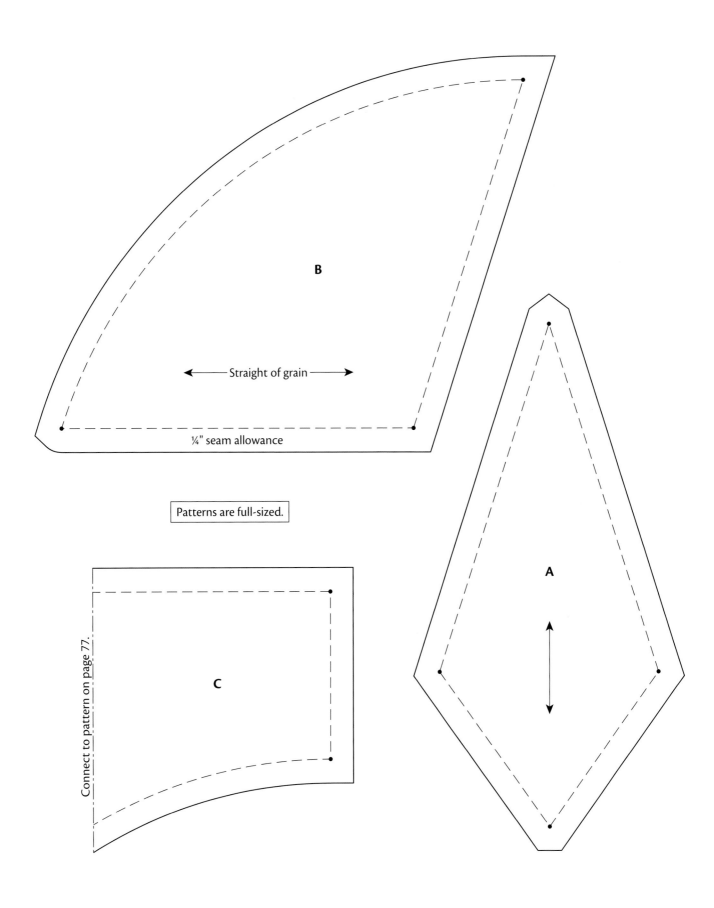

B

Straight of grain

¼" seam allowance

Patterns are full-sized.

Connect to pattern on page 77.

C

A

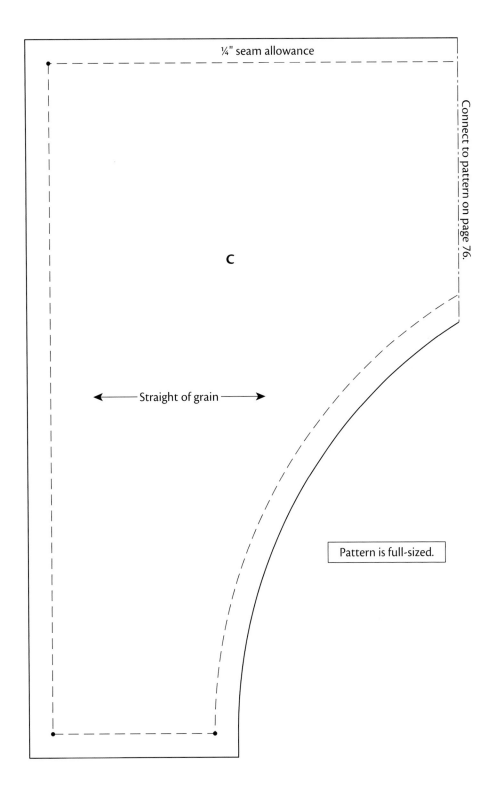

¼" seam allowance

Connect to pattern on page 76.

C

Straight of grain

Pattern is full-sized.

Maize-and-Blue Quilt

A wide range of blues, soft buttery yellows, golds, and tans give this quilt a universal appeal. The zigzag setting strips and flying-geese border add extra pizzazz. The block, called Our Editor, was found in **Once More around the Block** *by Judy Hopkins (Martingale & Company, 2003).*

Materials

All yardages are based on 42"-wide fabric.

5 yards *total* of assorted medium and dark blue prints for blocks and borders

4¾ yards *total* of assorted light, yellow, and gold prints for blocks and borders

2 yards *each* of 2 dark fabrics for zigzag setting strips

⅝ yard of medium blue print for outer pieced border

⅞ yard of fabric for binding

9⅝ yards of fabric for backing

105" x 105" piece of batting

A Note about the Borders

To simplify the fitting of the outer pieced borders, the directions include an additional ½" dark border before the final border of blue quarter-square triangles. This differs slightly from the quilt shown in the photograph.

Cutting

Since the blocks are scrappy, cutting is given for one block. Repeat the cutting for 25 blocks—23 full blocks and 4 half blocks. For ease of construction, the cutting for the 4 half blocks will produce two pairs of identical half blocks. This is slightly different from the quilt shown in the photograph, where the 4 half blocks are all different.

Cutting for One Block

From one light print, cut:

※ 1 square, 7¼" x 7¼"; cut twice diagonally to make 4 quarter-square triangles

※ 4 squares, 3⅞" x 3⅞"; cut each square once diagonally to make 8 half-square triangles

From one dark print, cut:

※ 1 square, 7¼" x 7¼"; cut twice diagonally to make 4 quarter-square triangles

※ 4 squares, 3⅞" x 3⅞"; cut each square once diagonally to make 8 half-square triangles

Cutting for the Remainder of the Quilt

From one dark print for zigzag setting strips, cut:

※ 6 squares, 18¼" x 18¼"; cut each square twice diagonally to make 24 quarter-square triangles. 2 are extra.

※ 3 squares, 9⅜" x 9⅜"; cut each square once diagonally to make 6 half-square triangles

Continued on page 81

Finished quilt: 99" x 99"

Finished block: 12" x 12"

Continued from page 79

**From the other dark print for
zigzag setting strips, cut:**

✳ 6 squares, 18¼" x 18¼"; cut each square twice
diagonally to make 24 quarter-
square triangles. 2 are extra.

✳ 3 squares, 9⅜" x 9⅜"; cut each square once
diagonally to make 6 half-square triangles

From the light prints, cut:

✳ 180 squares, 2⅞" x 2⅞"; cut each
square once diagonally to make 360
half-square triangles

✳ Cut the rest of the light prints into 1" strips
of random lengths. You will need at
least 800" of 1"-wide strips.

From the medium to dark blue prints, cut:

✳ 45 squares, 5¼" x 5¼"; cut each square twice
diagonally to make 180 quarter-square triangles

✳ 32 squares, 4¼" x 4¼"; cut each square twice
diagonally to make 128 quarter-square triangles

✳ Cut the rest of the dark prints into 1" strips of
random lengths. You will need at least
400" of 1"-wide strips.

**From the medium blue print
for outer border, cut:**

✳ 33 squares, 4¼" x 4¼"; cut each square twice
diagonally to make 132 quarter-square triangles

From the binding fabric, cut:

✳ 11 strips, 2¼" x 42"

Making the Blocks

1. Sew two pairs of light and dark quarter-square
triangles together as shown. Sew the pairs
together to make the center of the block.
Press.

2. Sew two light half-square triangles to a dark
quarter-square triangle as shown. Press. Make
two. Repeat to make two units with light
quarter-square triangles and dark half-square
triangles.

Make 2 of each.

3. Sew a light half-square triangle to a dark half-
square triangle. Make four. Press.

Make 4.

4. Arrange the units from steps 1–3 in rows as
shown; sew. Press. Repeat for a total of 23
blocks.

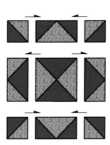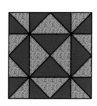

Make 23.

5. Make four half blocks as shown using the
remaining half-square and quarter-square triangles.

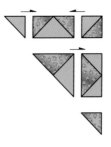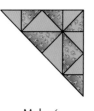

Make 4.

Assembling the Quilt Top

Arrange the blocks and setting triangles into five vertical rows as shown. Sew the blocks and triangles into rows; press toward the triangles, and then sew the rows together. Press the seam allowances to one side.

Assembling the Border

1. Sew the 1" light strips together so that you have eight strips of the following lengths: two 85½" strips, two 86½" strips, two 94½" strips, and two 95½" strips. Press the seam allowances to one side.

2. Sew the 85½" strips to the top and bottom of your quilt. Press the seam allowances toward the strips. Sew the two 86½" strips to the sides. Press toward the strips.

3. Sew a light 2⅞" half-square triangle to each side of a dark 5¼" quarter-square triangle. Press the seam allowances to one side. Repeat to make 180 flying-geese units for the borders.

Make 180.

4. Sew 43 of the flying-geese units into a strip. Press the seam allowances to one side. Repeat

to make another strip. Sew these strips to the sides of your quilt. The triangles should point toward the top on the left and to the bottom on the right.

Side.
Make 2.

5. Sew 47 of the flying-geese units into a strip. Note how the geese are arranged in the corners. Press the seam allowances to one side. Repeat for another strip.

Top

Bottom

6. Sew the strips from step 5 to the top and bottom of your quilt, making sure the triangles point in the correct direction. Press the seam allowances toward the narrow light border.

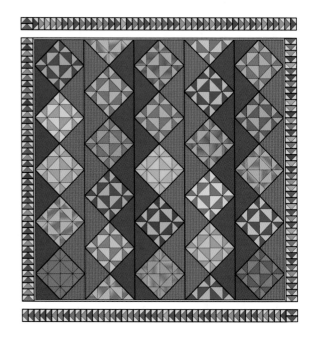

7. Sew the 1" x 94½" light strips to the top and bottom of your quilt. Press the seam allowances toward the strips.

8. Sew the 1" x 95½" strips to the sides of your quilt. Press toward the strips.

9. Sew the random-length 1" dark strips together to make two strips 95½" long and two strips 96½" long. Press the seam allowances in one direction.

10. Sew the 95½" dark strips to the top and bottom of your quilt. Press the seam allowances toward the strips. Sew the 96½" dark strips to the sides of the quilt. Press.

11. Sew 32 assorted medium to dark print and 33 medium blue print 4¼" quarter-square triangles into a strip, alternating the fabrics as shown. Repeat to make four strips. Press the seam allowances to one side.

Make 4.

12. Sew a strip from step 11 to each side of the quilt. Press the seam allowances toward the strips. Miter the diagonal seams at each corner; to do this, fold the quilt on the diagonal to align the raw edges. Begin sewing at the inside corner and stitch to the outer corner.

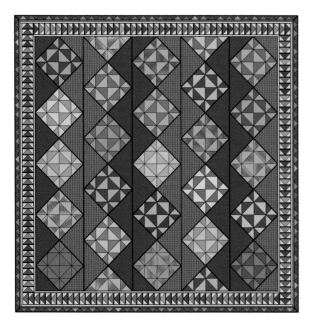

Finishing the Quilt

1. Cut the backing fabric into three sections approximately 42" x 108", 42" x 108", and 26" x 108". Sew together along the long edges and press the seam allowances open.

2. Center and layer the quilt top and batting over the backing; baste the layers together and quilt as desired.

3. Trim the backing and batting even with the quilt top. Use the 2¼" x 42" strips to bind the quilt referring to "Binding" (page 93).

4. Make a label and attach to the back of your quilt.

Quilting a Feather Vine

I quilted a meandering feather vine in the zigzag setting blocks. I didn't have a vine template, but I did have a feathered wreath template for a 12" block. I marked half of the feathered wreath in one setting triangle and then I flipped the template over and marked half of a feathered wreath in the next setting triangle. I had to fudge a bit where the ends met, but it worked very well. This also allowed me to mark as I went after the quilt was basted.

Quiltmaking Basics

I began quiltmaking many years ago when I discovered it combined two of my loves: fabric and handwork. I make my quilts by hand with a few exceptions. The Log Cabin blocks of "Old-Time Halloween Quilt" (page 44) were machine pieced and the string-pieced blocks of "Wild Wool Horses" (page 22) were machine pieced. Everything else in this book can be done by hand, and therefore can be taken with you. Often my quilts have never been near the sewing machine until the binding is ready to go on.

I always try to have a project available in a travel-ready state. This can be either a stack of precut pieces ready to be hand pieced or blocks ready for appliqué. In the classes that I teach, I hear of many creative strategies used by other fans of handwork. A lunch box or vintage make-up suitcase packed and ready to go with all your tools and fabric is a great idea. Blocks can be stitched as you commute on the bus or train, or on your lunch hour. I stitch during long car trips and children's sporting events. All of these projects, of course, can be done on the sewing machine, but don't be afraid to try one by hand. I think you will enjoy it.

Choosing Fabric for a Modern Antique

Use the following tips to help you achieve the look of the "modern antique."

Plaids, stripes, and other textural woven fabrics were used to great advantage years ago and are the easiest way to "age" your projects. They also provide a resting place for your eye when used with many printed fabrics.

There are wonderful antique reproduction fabrics in quilt shops now that have been extensively researched as to print, color, and era. The scholarship that fabric designers and manufacturers have put into the final product shows. They are exact duplicates or homages to fabric long gone. I love reproduction fabrics and use them copiously in my quiltmaking. I have found, though, that staying true to a particular era is less effective in making a quilt look old than choosing fabrics of many eras that have a particular vintage look.

As an example, in "Old-Time Halloween Quilt" I was trying to capture the look of an antique quilt that I saw at an antique folk-art show. The quilt was probably made in the 1920s because the fabrics were that age or earlier. What was most appealing to me was that it had faded quite a bit and this is what showed its age more than anything. Fabrics that were once black were now charcoal and other neutral shades. Some orange fabrics had faded to soft apricots. When reproducing the look of this quilt, I wanted fabrics that would appear as though they had once been black and orange, but were now something else entirely. When shopping for fabric and going through my stash, I tried to pick fabrics that reflected this characteristic. Of the many fabrics used in this quilt, only a few are true blacks and oranges. Most of them are my versions of "used-to-be black" and "used-to-be orange." In a nutshell, I used fabrics that were dark and drab for the blacks. For the orange, I used apricots, golds, tans, and some true oranges.

Nothing conveys age more than color. I find that using many shades of one color is more true to an old quilt than a uniform, dull, tea-dyed look. For example, many shades of red in a scrappy quilt mimic what happens in most antique quilts—the reds fade at different rates. Using many different scraps of one color will make your quilt look old more than anything else. This is because quiltmakers of the nineteenth century made their quilts using scraps—scrappy quilts are the easiest way to mimic age. I intuitively used this strategy to pick fabric for my quilts for some time. Once I began working with my sister, Polly Minick, who's a rug hooker, this strategy was really emphasized. Primitive rug hookers hand dye wool in many shades and textures of a particular color to mimic the old colors of a faded and worn antique rug. So, a practice I found intuitively was confirmed by other fiber artists trying to make antique reproductions. The highest praise I can get is "your quilts look so old."

Using Wool in Quilts

Many antique quilts were made of wool scraps and recycled wool clothing. They were practical, durable, and extremely warm. Several of the quilts in this book include wool. Don't be afraid to try sewing with it. You can use new wool or recycled wool.

Washing Your Wool

Vintage wool (recycled wool clothing) or new wool on the bolt must be washed and dried before you use it in a quilt, penny rug, or hooked rug. Wash your wool with like colors, as you would cotton, using a regular wash-and-dry cycle. Treat the wool as if it were a pair of jeans—wash in warm water and dry at a medium setting. Your wool will shrink up considerably, but it will be soft and fluffy and irresistible! Clean out the lint trap after every use because wool will produce a lot of lint. Occasionally you might want to wash and dry your wool twice if the first washing doesn't "full" up your wool significantly. Stay away from hot water and a hot dryer because you might get very thick wool felt and it will be too dense to quilt through.

Be sure to use 100% pure wool and not a wool blend or your wool will not "full" up when you wash and dry it.

Caring for a Wool Quilt

The type of wool used and how it is constructed will tell you how to launder your quilt. A wool quilt that is made completely from right-off-the-bolt wool that is not hand dyed can be washed in a washing machine if care is taken. All the wool was prewashed and dried, but it is possible that some of the wool could shrink further if heat and agitation are used in laundering. If the finished quilt is washed in cool water on a gentle cycle, spun out, and laid out flat to dry, then it can be washed.

A wool quilt that is a mixture of "as-is" wool (wool on the bolt) and hand-dyed wool can have the colors run when washed in the above manner. Any quilt with hand-dyed wool should only be dry-cleaned.

Tips for Working with Wool

1. All yardage requirements are generous and based on wool yardage *before* it is washed and dried. Wool will shrink quite a bit after washing and the amount of shrinkage varies greatly.

2. I like to use a sandpaper board when marking wool to hold the wool securely (see "Sandpaper board" on page 88). Wool tends to stretch and act like it is cut on the bias—even when it isn't! A sandpaper board is extremely effective when marking wool.

3. Wool won't be as responsive to pressing as cotton is. It has memory, which allows the fabric to spring back into its prior shape after pressing. When you press the seam allowances open, take this into consideration. The seam allowance won't iron completely flat. I use steam and press very carefully to avoid distortion.

4. When marking seam allowance dots on wool, use a Sharpie permanent marker. Use a delicate touch so only a very small dot shows. Test on scrap wool to see how much pressure is needed. Use only as much pressure as needed to mark on the wrong side to prevent the ink from showing on the front. I have found that Sharpie markers show up on wool very well. Traditional marking pencils may or may not be successful. Experiment—if a chalk or graphite pencil shows up on your wool, by all means use it. The Sharpie marker comes in many colors, so use the ink color that works best on your wool. Unfortunately, an ink dot that leaks onto the front side of your wool will be permanent.

5. Hand piecing wool is easy and effective. I recommend a medium-weight cotton thread (YLI Select is a good choice) and long needles. Use whatever needle is comfortable to you: hand appliqué, small embroidery, or milliner's. If you choose to machine piece, use a walking foot to help ease the bulk of the wool.

Supplies

I won't go into all the supplies needed to make a quilt. They are covered extensively in other books. This section will emphasize particular tools or supplies that are needed for handwork.

Needles. For hand piecing and appliqué, use a long, thin needle: a size 11 or 12 Sharp, size 12 appliqué needle, or a milliner's needle. For quilting, use Betweens, which are much shorter and easy to manipulate with the quilting stitch.

Thread. I recommend 100%-cotton thread for piecing, appliqué, and hand quilting. For piecing, a particular favorite of mine is YLI Select brand. It's much like hand-quilting thread in texture, but is a bit thinner and lighter so it's not bulky in the seams. It has more body than 100%-cotton all-purpose thread and therefore can be easily threaded in a needle. For appliqué, I like 100%-cotton thread made for machine embroidery, such as DMC brand. It comes in many colors and is practically invisible after it is sewn. Many quilters who do appliqué like to use silk thread, which is also very effective in achieving invisible stitches. It does tend to fray where it goes through the eye of the needle, though. Use short lengths to prevent wear. For hand quilting, I like YLI brand hand-quilting thread, because it never tangles and rarely requires a needle threader.

Appliqué glue. I find that Roxanne's appliqué glue (Roxanne's Glue-Baste-It), used as described on the packaging, is more efficient than appliqué pins. There are no pins to catch your thread as you sew. Use a fabric-glue stick for wool appliqué.

Appliqué pins. Use them for appliqué, if you prefer, and for English paper piecing.

Bias-tape maker. This handy notion makes quick work of bias stems. The finished bias width needed for "Fiesta Quilt" is ½". Cut bias strips 1" wide and feed them into the ½" bias maker. A folded, finished tape comes out the other end. Press the bias immediately and it is ready to be appliquéd.

Sandpaper board. This is used to stabilize cloth for marking prior to hand piecing and appliqué. When fabric is laid onto a sandpaper board, you can mark with less pressure and the fabric stays put. To make one, glue fine-grade sandpaper onto a hard work surface such as wood or acrylic.

Marking tools. I have a large collection of marking tools since different fabrics require different markers. The most useful are graphite pencils, silver marking pencils, and chalk pencils in several colors. Be sure to keep all pencils sharp so your marked lines are thin and accurate. Masking tape in many widths is very useful for marking straight quilting lines on your top. A Hera marker is useful also. It's a hard plastic tool much like a bone folder that puts a crease in your fabric instead of a penciled line. A Sharpie fine-point marker is effective when marking wool. It is a good idea to test all marking tools on fabric scraps before you begin your project to make certain that the marks can be removed when needed.

Batting. The desired look of the finished quilt and the ease of quilting are the most important factors to consider when choosing batting. For hand quilting, I prefer Hobbs 100% Organic Unbleached Cotton Batting because the finished washed quilt will most resemble an antique quilt. I also love Hobbs 100% Wool Batting for its ease in needling. This is especially helpful if you are quilting a top with many seams or appliqué layers. Wool, contrary to my first impression, takes up very little bulk when needling. The difference between the two is that a washed quilt with cotton batting will shrink and pucker around each quilting stitch to give it an old look. The wool batting, if washed as recommended, will not shrink.

Hand Piecing

The following steps provide information on how to hand piece.

1. Rotary cut fabric pieces with an added ¼" seam allowance, just as for machine piecing. Lay the cut piece on a sandpaper board to keep the fabric from distorting and to reduce pressure on the marking tool. Use a 1" x 12" acrylic ruler and a marking pencil to mark a scant ¼" (to take the width of the marked line into account) around all edges on the wrong side of each piece. The marked line is your sewing line.

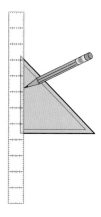

2. Align two pieces along the raw edges, right sides together. I like to use a Sharp or milliner's needle and YLI Select thread. Don't knot the thread at the end; instead, take a small backstitch on top of your first stitch to secure it. Start and stop at the points where the marked lines intersect, using a running stitch (about ¹⁄₁₆" long) on the line. Do not sew into the seam allowance. Check occasionally to be

sure you're sewing on the marked line on both the front and the back. Also, take a backstitch every 1" to 1½".

3. To end the sewing line, take a small stitch on top of your last stitch and then make a knot in your thread. Pull the knot down with your fingernail so that it is right against the fabric, and pull to secure it. When you reach an intersection of seam lines, make an extra stitch to anchor your pieces.

Hand Appliqué

Needle-turn appliqué is my preferred appliqué method. Since so little preparation is required, I think it is the most time-efficient method—and the most portable. Please note that the appliqué templates do not include seam allowances. Add a seam allowance when cutting them from cotton fabric. For wool appliqué, cut the fabric exactly on the marked line. Wool does not need to be turned under because washed wool does not fray.

1. Draw around the appliqué template on the right side of your cotton fabric to mark your sewing line. Cut ⅛" from this line.

2. Use a few drops of appliqué glue to hold the piece in place on the background fabric, or use pins.

3. Thread an appliqué or milliner's needle with thread that matches the appliqué and knot

the end. Starting on a straight edge or a gentle curve, use the tip of the needle to turn under the seam allowance on the marked line. Turn under only about ½" ahead of where your needle comes up, just enough for only the next four or five stitches. Work from right to left if you are right-handed and hold the turned seam allowance between the thumb and forefinger of your left hand. If you are left-handed, work from left to right and hold the work in your right hand. Note: a seam allowance that will be covered by another piece does not need to be turned under.

4. Bring the needle up through the background fabric and into the crease of the seam allowance of the appliqué piece; pull the thread taut. Insert the needle into the background directly next to where it came into the appliqué piece. Let the needle travel about ¹⁄₁₆" to the left of the previous stitch and again come up into the crease of the folded edge (or a thread or two into the appliqué piece). Keep your stitches snug, but don't pull so tightly that the fabric puckers.

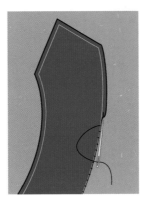 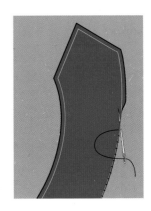

5. To end the stitching, pull the needle to the wrong side of the fabric. Take two small stitches into the background fabric behind the appliqué piece. Don't let these stitches show on the front. Make a knot and clip the thread, leaving a ½" tail.

No Pins

Using a water-soluble appliqué glue such as Roxanne's Glue-Baste-It instead of pins is my favorite way to adhere appliqué pieces into place. There is nothing to get tangled with your sewing thread and the pieces lie very flat. Only a few tiny dots of glue are needed, and it will not affect the ease of your hand quilting. Once your quilt is completed and washed, the glue will disappear.

Appliquéing Outside Points

Begin by taking smaller stitches closer together when you approach an outside point. When you reach the point, take a stitch directly at the point, and use the tip of your needle to push the seam allowance under it and toward the side already sewn. Trim away some of the seam allowance, if necessary, for a perfect point. Continue to stitch the next side as before.

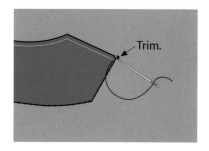

Trim.

Appliquéing Inside Points

You will need to clip the seam allowance into the point so that you can turn the fabric under on each side of the point. Then, when approaching an inside point, start taking smaller, closer stitches about ¼" before the point. Stitch past the point, return, and make another stitch at the point, stitching into the appliqué piece a few more threads to hold it securely.

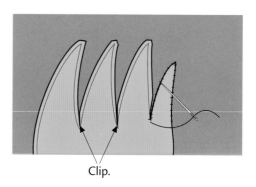

Clip.

Reverse Appliqué

Reverse appliqué is just as easy as regular appliqué, so don't be intimidated. In fact, it's often easier to use this technique, which involves cutting away part of the top fabric to let the fabric underneath show, rather than trying to appliqué a small shape on top. Here is how to reverse appliqué using the outline curves of the pitcher in "Fiesta Quilt" (page 52) as an example.

1. Before cutting the pitcher shape, baste the dark red pitcher fabric on top of the light red fabric.

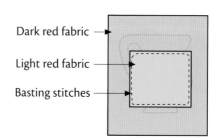

Dark red fabric

Light red fabric

Basting stitches

2. Cut a slit into the curved area marked on the top fabric; this will be where the highlight on the pitcher shows through the darker fabric. Cut only the top fabric, not the lighter background fabric. Cut a V-shaped snip at each end of the marked curve.

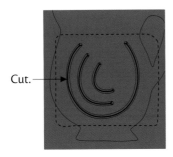

Cut. →

3. With your needle, tuck each side of the highlight area under until the fabric is pushed under the drawn line. Appliqué on this line all the way around as you would for regular appliqué, turning the seam under with the needle as you go.

4. After all the reverse appliqué is complete, turn the appliqué block to the back and remove the basting stitches. Carefully cut away the light red underneath fabric from the areas where it is still behind the top fabric, leaving a ¼" seam allowance. This will make your block lighter, more flexible, and easier to quilt through.

Embroidery Stitches

Some of the quilts in this book have embroidery details. The specific stitches are shown below.

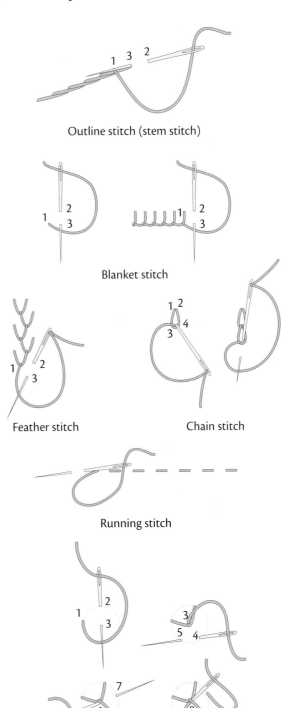

Outline stitch (stem stitch)

Blanket stitch

Feather stitch

Chain stitch

Running stitch

Spiderweb stitch

Marking the Quilt Top

After your top is complete and you have decided on a quilting design, mark the design onto your quilt top with a marking tool that can be washed away after your quilt is finished. Refer to "Marking tools" (page 88) for suggested marking tools and make sure you test any marker on fabric scraps before using it.

When I look at a finished quilt top and decide how it will be quilted, I then decide how it will be marked. If possible, I mark the top after it has been basted, and I mark in small areas at a time so I will not need to mark again. I quilt in a hoop, and if I mark the whole top before it is basted, the marks will wear off during the handling of the quilt. If you are going to quilt in a floor frame, it can be completely marked before it is basted.

When I want to use a design I don't have a stencil for (either a purchased stencil or a home-made one), such as an intricate feather wreath or an odd-sized design, I will mark this section on the top *before* it is basted using a light box. Often the quilting designs I use are a combination of markings put on a top before it is basted and markings after it is basted. The disadvantage of marking a top before it is basted (using a light box) is that you cannot mark again using a light box after it is basted if your marks rub off.

My strategy for quilting a top that has both kinds of designs (marked before and after basting) is that I quilt the marked areas first, before the marks have a chance to rub off. Once this quilting is done I mark the remaining quilting designs as I go.

I have collected many stencils over the years, both purchased and homemade, so I don't have the need to mark beforehand too often. It is much easier to mark as you go, and my quilting designs are often chosen with this in mind.

Marking without Pencils

A Hera marker is a wonderful way to mark an allover fan quilting design (see "Marking tools" on page 88). The Hera marker will make a sharp crease in the fabric instead of a lead or chalked line. You won't ever have to worry about your pencil mark not washing out. The crease will naturally disappear in a few days or so. Mark only a day's worth of quilting at one time.

Layering and Basting the Quilt

After you've marked the top, layer the top, batting, and backing into a quilt "sandwich." The quilt backing and batting must be at least 3" larger on all sides than the quilt top. If the backing is pieced, press the seam allowances open for easier quilting.

1. Spread the backing, wrong side up, on a clean flat surface. Secure the edges with masking tape. Keep the back smooth, but do not stretch it too tightly.

2. Spread the batting over the backing, smoothing out any wrinkles. Lay the quilt top over the batting, right side up, and smooth it out. Keep the quilt-top edges square with the backing and backing.

3. Baste the layers together with needle and thread, rustproof safety pins, or a basting spray (following the manufacturer's directions). When basting with thread or pins, do so in a large grid pattern spaced every 6" to 8". I also like to baste all the way around the perimeter

of the quilt, approximately ¼" from the edge, to keep the edges square and secure.

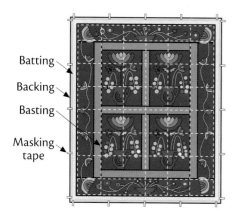

Batting
Backing
Basting
Masking tape

Hand Quilting

1. Thread a quilting needle (called a Between) with about 18" of hand-quilting thread and make a small knot at the end of the thread. Insert the needle into the top layer of the quilt, about ½" from where you want to start the quilting stitches. Push the needle through the top and batting (but not the backing). Bring the needle up at the quilting line. Gently tug on the thread until the knot pops through the fabric and is buried in the quilt batting.

2. Make small, even running stitches on the marked quilting line through all the quilt layers.

3. To end your quilting thread, place the needle next to the point where the quilting thread comes out of the quilt. Wrap the thread around the needle three times. Insert the needle back into the quilt top and batting (but not the backing), one stitch-length away. Bring the needle up approximately ½" away and gently tug on the quilting thread until the knot you made is buried in the quilt batting. Clip the thread.

For more instructions on hand quilting, read *Loving Stitches: A Guide to Fine Hand Quilting* by Jeana Kimball (Martingale & Company, 2003).

Binding

Once you've finished quilting your quilt, trim the batting and backing even with the quilt top. To make a straight-grain binding, cut enough 2¼"-wide strips to go around all sides of your quilt plus an extra 6" to 8". Join the strips in a continuous length using a diagonal seam to help distribute bulk. Pressing the seam allowances open will also help reduce the bulk.

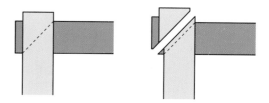

1. Cut one end of the strip at a 45° angle, fold the raw edge over ¼", and press. Fold the strip in half lengthwise with the wrong sides together; press. Starting at one side of the quilt (not at the corner), sew the binding to the quilt front using a ¼" seam allowance. Leave about 4" unsewn at the beginning. Stop stitching ¼" from the corner of the quilt. Backstitch and cut the thread.

¼"
Binding strip
Quilt top

2. Turn the quilt so that you can sew along the next side. Fold the binding up away from the quilt at a 45° angle. Fold the binding back down upon itself. There will be a triangle of

excess binding at the corner that will create a miter.

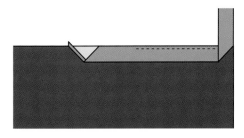

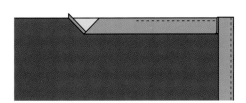

3. Begin to stitch again along the next side of the quilt, again using a ¼" seam allowance. Backstitch at the beginning to secure your stitches, but stop stitching ¼" from the next corner of the quilt.

4. Repeat the process for each corner. When you are within 3" to 4" of the beginning of the binding, tuck the ending into the beginning of the binding and trim the excess. Finish stitching the binding to the quilt.

5. Fold the binding over the raw edge of the quilt and sew the folded edge to the quilt back using an appliqué stitch. A miter will form naturally at each corner as you fold the binding into place.

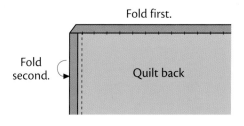

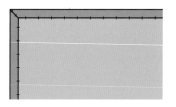

Labeling the Quilt

It's important to label your quilt so the recipient and future generations will know the story behind it. You can make a plain fabric label, or you can repeat a design or block from the front of the quilt, as I often like to do. Use a permanent fabric marker (or embroidery stitches) to sign your name, date, and any other pertinent information about your quilt on the label. Appliqué the label onto the back of your quilt.

Resources

Halcyon Yarn
1-800-341-0282
www.halcyonyarn.com
Matte pearl cotton (Homestead Cotton)

Hobbs Bonded Fibers
1-800-433-3357
www.hobbsbondedfibers.com
Wool and cotton quilt batting

Marlene Dusbiber
1-734-475-2159
www.marlenedusbiber.com
Carved wooden chickens

Martingale & Company
1-800-426-3126
www.martingale-pub.com
Papers for foundation piecing

Paper Pieces
1-800-337-1537
www.paperpieces.com
Paper hexagons for English paper piecing

United Notions and Moda Fabrics
1-800-527-9447
www.modafabrics.com
Prairie cloth and 100% wool

The Wool Street Journal
1-888-784-5667
www.woolstreetjournal.com
Wool-stitching and rug-hooking magazine

YLI Corporation
1-803-985-3100
www.ylicorp.com
Thread for hand quilting and hand piecing

About the Author

A lifelong needle artist, Laurie's quilts grace galleries and private collections and have been featured in *Country Home, Coastal Living, Architectural Digest, American Patchwork and Quilting, McCall's Quilting,* and the *Wool Street Journal.*

A patchwork quilt in a magazine inspired Laurie to take up quilting at the age of 14. Drawn to traditional themes and techniques, she pieces, appliqués, and quilts by hand. "Handwork is calming and meditative. It's the way I was meant to work," says Laurie. She joyfully spends her time quilting, creating, teaching, writing, and designing fabric with her sister and design partner, Polly Minick. Visit their Web site: www.minickandsimpson.com.

Laurie lives with her husband, Bill, in Ann Arbor, Michigan. They share their home with a happy menagerie of two cats and a dog.